Ann Ree Colton, 1947.

PROPHET FOR THE ARCHANGELS

PROPHET FOR THE ARCHANGELS

by

ANN REE COLTON
and
JONATHAN MURRO

ARC PUBLISHING COMPANY
POST OFFICE BOX 1138
GLENDALE, CALIFORNIA 91209

SECOND PRINTING

Printed in the United States of America

Preface

Ann Ree Colton came into the world with the gift of second sight. Over the years she has become an enlightened prophet, a versatile revelator, an inspired initiate, and a talented teacher. As a prophet, her eyes perceive coming horizons; as a revelator, she reveals new truths and discloses the answers to age-old questions; as an initiate, she understands the initiatory processes of life; as a teacher, she knows the needs of the individual in search of spiritual fulfillment. Therefore, in addition to her prophecies and revelations, she is able to offer vital instruction pertaining to the practical issues of everyday life.

The test of a prophet and teacher is whether he can remain true to his spiritual gifts and inner guidance while he endures the hardships, meets the challenges, and overcomes the obstacles imposed by a resisting world. When I first met Ann Ree Colton in December 1951, the trials and tests of her earlier years were completed, and her fertile mind was beginning to tap a new stream of creative and prophetic thought. It is with reverence and humility that I extend prayerful gratitude to God for permitting me to accompany Ann Ree Colton during the magnificent years of her illumination. In these golden years she has written profound and powerful books, and has founded a unique system of spiritual ethics and techniques appropriately designed for persons of faith who live in a scientific age.

After a serious heart condition almost ended her life in 1961, Ann Ree Colton made a dedication to work with me on her biography. For some time I had hoped that she would write a book of her spiritual memoirs, as many persons have wondered about the salient experiences that have motivated her life as a prophet and teacher. I began work on the first chapters of the book in 1962, using for reference the reminiscent comments she had spoken to me over the past ten years. The following summer, while working together on the remaining chapters, we observed that the manuscript was developing into a combined biography and autobiography. We then proceeded to write the book as co-authors, with her autobiographical comments printed in italics.

I have received many blessings during the preparation of this volume—for to research the spiritual life of a true prophet and teacher is to discover a vast treasury of wisdom; it is to voyage into the realm of the future; it is to raise the curtain between Heaven and earth.

JONATHAN MURRO

Contents

Acknowledgments

Sincere thanks are hereby extended to Anastasia Wilson and Alban McRoberts for their typing and editing assistance, and to Serena Burris and Tobias De-Marchi for their editing suggestions.

Illustrations

Kabalistic painting, titled *Music.* The Music of the Spheres became audible to Ann Ree through this painting.

Kabalistic painting, *Christ is Risen.* Painted during Easter, 1930.

Ann Ree, 1942.

1944.

In the chapel in Florida, 1950.

Following page 262.

Ann Ree conducting the first Guild of Ethics, November 1, 1956. Glendale, California.

Sculptured Head of Jesus, titled *But I Say Unto You.* By Ann Ree, 1956.

The Garment of Jesus. Painted by Ann Ree, 1957. Design for mosaic mural (86″ x 70″) in the Glendale chapel.

The Holy Family. Design for a mosaic mural, 1959.

Ann Ree with four of the Niscience Lay Ministers.

In the garden at Foundation Headquarters, Glendale, California.

Ann Ree christening Eleanor "Liebschien" Muusmann, 1963.

July 1963. Ann Ree Colton and Jonathan Murro in Santa Barbara, California. Behind them is the glide-swing used at Wooded Place in 1953.

Ann Ree teaching the *Dear Child Round Table,* Glendale, 1964.

Introduction

Four daughters and a son were born to Harriette and Emory Whitaker of Atlanta, Georgia. Their second child, Ann Ree, was born in Atlanta on August 17, 1898. Emory Whitaker came from a family of English and Irish origin, his ancestors settling in America in the year of 1633. His wife, born Harriette Mitchell, was descended from Scotch, Welsh and English ancestry; the Mitchell family also came to America in the seventeenth century.

The Whitaker and Mitchell families made their fortunes in early America as shipbuilders and shipowners. Both families later became landowners in the South. After the Civil War the Whitakers and the Mitchells lost their wealth, but retained their land. During her childhood Ann Ree was a constant visitor to the Mitchell plantation, fifteen miles south of Atlanta.

One of Ann Ree's great-uncles was a Governor of Georgia and the founder of Lucy Cobb College. Among her other relatives were a Judge of the Supreme Court of Georgia, a member of the State legislature, a prominent railroad official, and a bank founder. Her father was a supervisor of mechanical installations.

Her mother and grandmother were among the heirs named to inherit a large fortune that had been deposited in the chancery of England. This fortune was forfeited to the Crown of England when other relatives refused to accept the terms of the inheritance. It was not the destiny of Ann Ree to have a background of material wealth; it was the destiny of her soul, however, to inherit spiritual riches from Heaven.

J. M.

1

The Early Years

I love them that love me; and those that seek me early shall find me.

—Proverbs 8:17

Legend has it that a baby born in a caul is especially blessed, and will bring good luck to others. It is believed that one born in a caul will have second sight, and also provident protection, particularly protection from drowning. Some persons believe that caul babies stand a good chance of becoming saints.

Harriette Wheeler, who assisted in the delivery of her great-granddaughter, Ann Ree, was excited when she saw that a caul covered the head of the baby. The Negro servants in the Mitchell household, where the birth took place, were jubilant about the caul. Harriette Whitaker, the mother of the baby, felt differently about the caul. She did not want to believe that her child would have supernatural powers.

In Ann Ree's early years, when she began to speak of her visions and unseen playmates, she was punished by her mother, for her mother was strongly determined that Ann Ree be not different from her other children.

Perhaps it was her memory of the caul that caused Harriette Whitaker to be so violently against her daughter's visions.

The cause of Ann Ree's difficulty was that she did not know how to distinguish between what she saw in vision and what she saw in the physical world. Because she was punished often and severely, due to her second sight, these stern reprovings during her childhood were to graft in the feeling of guilt toward her visions—a feeling that would continue until her middle years.

When persons are endowed with timely spiritual gifts, their training in the use of these gifts is under the direction of Heaven. For Ann Ree, this training began in her fourth year. One day, while the little girl was resting on a couch in her grandmother's living room, her attention was drawn to the geometrical symbols on a stained glass window, and she had the experience of *knowing* what the symbols of the square and the triangle represented. This was the first time she realized that when her eyes looked upon anything with a certain fixity, the object projected its meaning to her. It was also the beginning of an awareness which was to increase through the years. In time she was to become an adept interpreter of the language of symbology.

When Ann Ree was five years old, she began to see visions of two kindly eyes. Whenever the eyes appeared, she felt loved and protected. If she were sad, the eyes would gaze at her comfortingly; if she had not been good, they would look at her sorrowfully.

In her sixth year Ann Ree was punished quite severely after she told her mother about speaking with an uncle who had been dead for two days. Her mother accused her of "just making it up." However, Ann Ree could not deny her conversation with her deceased uncle. He was very real to her, and she could not understand why she was not believed.

Before school began to extend her mind, Ann Ree was gathering an education of another kind. She became aware of the many superstitions and beliefs of the local Negroes. Many times she saw them hang their conjure bags on their clotheslines and under the eaves of their homes. Whatever the Negroes did that was connected with voodoo repelled the little girl, for she intuited that such practices were tinged with evil.

It was in her sixth year that Ann Ree asked her mother and father for permission to attend the churches of her own choice. This request came not from curiosity, but from the hunger to find a spiritual home. Her parents, having no religious prejudices, gave her this freedom. During the next several years she visited the many different churches in the adjoining communities, often returning to those in which she would find peace.

The overshadowing spiritual protection that was to follow Ann Ree manifested itself clearly in her sixth year, when she was healed of a severe case of poison oak. After a number of different lotions and remedies, offered by relatives and neighbors, had failed to bring relief, the sick little girl was inspired to bathe in the ocean. On the following morning there was no remaining trace of poison oak.

My cousins and some neighbor boys "double-dog-dared" me to rub poison oak on my face, neck and ears. The result was painful and ludicrous. My face swelled in a balloon-like fashion, and I was delirious for several days. When the time arrived for my family to take our annual Jacksonville Beach vacation, I was still a frightful-appearing child. My face was so swollen that I could not wear my hat. To my mortification, my mother put a sunbonnet on me, and to make matters worse, my cousins who accompanied us called me "Old Poison Oak." When I reached the beach I received an inner prompting which told me to go into the water and I would be healed. I remained in the water for a long time. The next day there was no sign of poison oak on my face or body.

At the age of seven Ann Ree was guided by an inner voice to obtain a glass of water, sit near a lamp, become very quiet, and look deeply into the water. When she followed this direction, the water would begin to grow very clear, and there would appear either pastoral scenes or great white buildings surrounded by blue and gold. This was her first experience in the use of extended sight in a deliberate manner, and also the beginning of her seeing etheric pictures and symbols in every form of life. Her training with the glass of water lasted less than one month, but it was the beginning of her realization that all that happens or may happen in the earth is mirrored through the elements of Nature.

The love of teaching began in her eighth year. In an empty room in her home, she set up a blackboard and chairs, and taught Bible stories to the neighborhood white and colored children. At the conclusion of each session of Bible reading, teaching, and prayer, she would baptize their willing heads with a bucket of water. Her parents, relatives, and mature friends would often comment upon her understanding of the Holy Bible.

Judge T. E. Whitaker, of the Georgia Supreme Court, called his niece "sweet little Ann Ree." The members of her immediate family called her "Ree." Emory Whitaker said to a friend, "Ree is the best child I have, but don't ever get her mad." He knew that his daughter was provoked to anger whenever she saw injustice inflicted upon the weak.

The Civil War had forced many Southerners into a vegetarian diet due to the absence of animals. As meat became plentiful in the years after the war, some of these Southerners and their children retained their vegetarian diets. Ann Ree's parents were among those who preferred to set a vegetarian table. In their home was always an abundance of fresh vegetables, fruit, and milk. Fish was served for Sunday morning breakfast. No stimulants were ever served.

The games Ann Ree liked best were the ones that came out of her own imagination. In one of these games she would play the part of a nun who was putting up a ladder to escape over the walls of a convent. Those friends who did not care for this type of imaginative play would say, "You're not a nun. I'm not a nun. And anyway we're not Catholics."

Many years later it was revealed to her that she had lived more than one life in a cloister, and in one of these lives she actually did scale the walls of a convent during a period of unbearable corruption and deception. She learned that some of her other childhood imaginative experiences also came from former-life memories. In her adult years, when she researched the inner life of children, Ann Ree saw the confirmation of her own conviction that the field of imagery which feeds each child's imaginative process is colored by former lives, and that children often dramatize their previous lives in their childhood games, particularly before their twelfth year. Knowing this, she was able to help hundreds of mothers to have a better relating with their children through the understanding of their children's former-life backgrounds.

In her ninth year Ann Ree went with her friends to the circus, where they witnessed with fascination the act of an acrobat. On returning home she stretched a rope between two trees, and startled her companions by successfully duplicating some of the professional performer's difficult feats. This was one of the first times she was conscious of the fact that she could draw on a source of unusual strength or energy which enabled her to accomplish whatever she set her mind and will to do.

One day while the young girl was standing in front of the State Capitol building in Atlanta, her attention was drawn to a church placard containing a saying of Jesus written in golden letters. When her eyes fell upon the words, "Ye shall know the truth, and the truth shall make you free," the words pierced her heart, and she burst into uncontrollable sobbing. This moving experience with the words of Jesus made a gateway into her soul—and throughout her life she was never to lose touch with the reality of Jesus. From childhood on, she knew Him to be the Saviour, the Lord of the human heart.

Throughout Ann Ree's early years books were to play an important part in her development. Even before attending school she had become an avid reader, and, as she grew older, rarely was she seen without a book of some kind in her hands. When adult friends noticed that she possessed a mature discrimination in her choice and selection of books, she was given access to several private libraries, including the library of a minister who encouraged her in her reading and studying.

Ann Ree showed a special interest in books of an historical nature, particularly biographies. When such books correlated to the history of her own former lives, they would often stir the memories of those times within her. However, she would have to await a future day for the spiritual confirmation and intellectual clarification of her intuitions pertaining to past lives.

In her ninth year Ann Ree was presented with a number of old books salvaged from a fire. The unexpected gift included the book *Quo Vadis*. As she read this book about early Christian times, she identified herself with the pain, anguish and glory of the martyrs, and her dreams for many nights were colored by terrifying sounds and sights. Much later in her life she was to learn that she had lived during the period of early Christianity and had suffered martyrdom then, and in other lives to follow.

Those who recognized Jesus as the world Saviour while He was in the physical world were in alignment with His Saviourship; because they were part of Him, they attracted certain martyrdom to themselves. Some of these persons are in the world today, and they now have, as compensation for such former lives in which they were singled out for martyrdom, spiritual gifts and powers. In the present period they work to sustain the note of world-grace for the masses, and to free the Christ-Light onto a new spiral in earth. Those now living in the world who were not singled out for martyrdom—but who suffered in the mass persecutions of Christians—have, as compensation, access to a deeper spiritual understanding.

The gift of salvaged books was the beginning of a long series of similar happenings in which books came into Ann Ree's hands through seeming acts of Providence. Time after time, a book correlating to some inner experience was placed in her hands *after* she had the experience; as an indirect instruction, the book would confirm and clarify what she had experienced inwardly. There were also times when a book somehow paralleling an inner experience would come into her possession, perfectly timed to her need.

During her ninth year Ann Ree experienced for the first time the sensation of moving out of her physical body. She was never frightened or disturbed by this sensation.

I did not know how I did it, but I loved to do it. At first, I would fly about my bedroom, touching the ceiling and walls, fully conscious and aware of what I was doing.

Many persons remember "flying" in their dreams at night, but to command this ability in the waking state is a skill known only to a few. The childhood experience of releasing herself from her physical body was used by Ann Ree with no outer or inner explanation. Later in her life, however, the spiritual understanding of this gift was revealed to her. She learned that only those who have had a skilled use of the *higher etheric body* in former lives may have access to its use as early as the ninth year in the present life. Thus, they are able to begin etheric-flight experience without harm to the glandular system.

The higher etheric body is the everlasting body which survives death. When this body is released from the physical body, one has the power to rise above the confinement of gravity.

The ability to release herself from her physical body while she was fully awake on her bed at night, and to fly undisturbed and undismayed in the confines of the bedroom, was to continue from her ninth year to her fourteenth year. The sensation of flying did not occur again until her twenty-first year; when it returned, she was conscious of the ability to take flight over cities and into buildings while her physical body was thousands of miles away. After certain initiatory experiences in her twenty-third year, she learned how to rise in her higher etheric body to the many diversified degrees of light accompanying the earth. Therefore, it was to be her destiny as a spiritual server to explore and research the invisible regions, planes, spheres, realms and kingdoms.

In her ninth year etheric pageants of sorrow or joy began to appear on the walls of her room. She soon learned that these etheric pageants were being used to tell her whether the days ahead would include an unpleasant experience or a happy event. Those who were giving her these warnings and love-assurances were the same ones who never refused her requests for help;

she addressed them as "my beloveds." There was a "special one" upon whom she could depend—the one who revealed only his eyes. The others had faces and vapor-like, fluidic forms that were more distinct and recognizable. If doleful or sad expressions were on the faces, she was being warned of some unhappy incident soon to occur in her life. Smiling or happy faces would invariably predict a cause for joy.

She knew that these loving and kind ones were living, yet were not of the world, and that they were definitely not death entities; for she had already had a few frightening experiences with death apparitional entities. Apparitional entities are the *unrisen dead* who have the power to make themselves seen by one living in the world.

The protective grace represented by the etheric pageants and faces was merely one phase of her early evolvement. As she approached maturity, there manifested other forms or types of guidance of a more direct nature.

In her ninth year Ann Ree was shown in a vision that her future husband would speak a different language and would come from far across the sea.

From her ninth year to her eleventh year she spent whatever days she could in the neighboring woods, especially when it rained. These sojourns in the woods always started at dogwood blossom time and ended with the goldenrods in the autumn, when the wild fox grapes were in the trees and lush berries were along the banks of the creek. The massive oaks and pines, the dogwood, the sweetgum, the sassafras tree; the wild hickory nuts, hazelnuts, black walnuts; the laurel, the broomsage, the fennel, the pungent budded sweetshrub, the snakeplant; the wild violets, the goldenrod—all filled her with the wonder of God. In this environment she first talked with the Nature beings, who instructed her how to arrange dry branches and leaves into a tepee-like shelter. Here, the Nature beings taught her how to ripen plums more quickly, and how to help calves when they are sick.

My mother was a domestic agrarian. We were always surrounded by domestic animals and had a tillable garden plot to supplement our table. It was my responsibility to raise a certain number of calves. I learned much from these bovine pets and they flourished under my care.

In Georgia the plums are slow to ripen. The Nature beings taught me how to push forward the ripening of the plums. They told me to put the plums in the dark earth about sixteen inches deep, and in ten days I would find them to be a red harvest of tasteful fruit. I found that plums ripened in this manner were more delicious than the fruit plucked from the trees.

In the years ahead Ann Ree was to reach a close affinity with Nature and, eventually, a comprehensive understanding of the Nature beings, the angels, and the great Intermediaries who work through Nature.

During her childhood contacts with Nature, she became acquainted with a beautifully-clothed, etheric maiden, whom she called "my invisible friend." The maiden taught her about plants, trees, the moss on rocks, and about the curative effect of certain herbs, berries, and grasses. She taught Ann Ree how to build a wooded nest out of pine branches so as to keep out the rain. She taught her the rain music, and told her about the music of the small creeks and waters. The etheric maiden taught her things about the earth, and taught her lessons of the wind and the sun.

Over forty years later Ann Ree was to discover that the maiden was, in reality, a vision and memory of a former life in which she had lived during the time of Atlantis. The memory of this past life or embodiment was cast forth by her soul so that she could recall the Atlantean days when—as a maiden named "TiSeila"—she was trained by the Devas, who taught her many of Nature's secrets.

From her childhood experiences with the etheric maiden, Ann Ree gained her first knowledge of the use of the will through the akasic fluid centered within the adrenal glands—knowledge that later would sustain her through tremendous ordeals and trials. This remnant of memory from Atlantean times gave her the clue to the type of will used in Atlantis, when the will was used in a manner yet to be recovered by men. In rare instances today, this use of the will is tapped by persons during periods of crisis, thereby enabling them to draw upon a mysterious inner source of extraordinary physical strength, vitality, and endurance.

It was later revealed to Ann Ree that she was permitted to recall the memory of the "TiSeila" embodiment because the Atlantean life correlated to her present life, and contained something that was needed to be added to this life. She learned that the etheric, formlike mold of an ancient embodiment is called an "archaic prototype shell." If the ancient embodiment is important or significant in transposing the knowledge from one age to another, the memory of the distant past is revealed—and the archaic prototype shell is dissolved and subtly incorporated into the consciousness of the present life.

Ann Ree's love for animals and the out-of-doors, and a determination to be self-reliant, motivated her to volunteer to do many heavy farm chores from her eleventh year through her fourteenth year. Without knowing it, she was preparing a strong physical body for the arduous road ahead, and was gaining a sympathetic accord with the animal kingdom. These activities helped her to avoid the dream stage that often accompanies adolescence, and fortified her with a practical viewpoint on life.

The first major turning point in her life occurred after she was stricken with typhoid fever in her fourteenth year. The family doctor did everything he could, but her condition grew steadily worse. For a brief moment Ann Ree awakened from a deep coma. Turning to her mother, she spoke slowly, "I will never get well. I will die. Send for Uncle Zack. He is the only one who can save me."

Zack Henry, a doctor in a village thirty miles away, answered the dying girl's request for his help. His advice and recommended treatment enabled his niece to pass safely through the crisis and to begin her recovery.

The direct guidance Ann Ree received as to the person who had the exact knowledge necessary to save her life was part of the infallible "knowing" which accompanies true inner perception. This inner knowing was later to be responsible for her aiding many others to reach the proper person or thing in the time of crisis and need.

While recuperating from her long siege with typhoid fever, Ann Ree received permission to attend church on Easter Sunday. It was the first time she had left her home since her illness, and being still weak, she walked slowly and shakily to church. When the fifteen-year-old girl arrived at the church, someone opened the large, heavy door for her. After entering the building, she pushed the door closed, but the latch failed to hold and the door was left slightly ajar. She noticed that the Easter service was being conducted by a new minister, rather than the minister-friend she had expected to see. As the young girl took her place in the congregation, the new minister stopped in the middle of a sentence and glared directly at her. He shouted angrily, "Go back and shut that door."

Ann Ree was embarrassed and shocked, for she thought the door was closed—and the minister's manner offended what she thought should be hospitality in a place of worship. She calmly went back and closed the door. However, instead of returning to her seat, she left the building, never to return again.

A few months later the miniature book *At the Feet of the Master* was placed in her hands. This little book confirmed what she knew inwardly, and was to be a guiding light until she met the Master face to face.

2

The Disciplinary Years

For many are called, but few are chosen.

—St. Matthew 22:14

Life has many paths from which one may choose. If one chooses a path that leads to the soul, his choice has come from a wellspring of innate wisdom. Even if he is young in years, this wellspring fortifies him with an excellent sense of spiritual direction.

In her sixteenth year Ann Ree made a decision that determined her future years. A motion picture director visiting Atlanta was impressed by her beauty and tried to persuade her to become interested in a career in motion pictures. Her intuition prompted her to decline the offer. What she wanted to do was already on her mind: she wanted to marry—and to raise a family. When her grandmother remarked about her wanting to marry so young, Ann Ree replied, "I have to have my children early because there is something else I must do in the world!"

A year before this, a musician named Alexander Taranko had arrived in Atlanta to organize the band for Georgia Tech, and to assemble and direct a symphony orchestra. The musician was a White Russian who had come to the United States in his fourteenth year, and had graduated from the Walter Damrosch Conservatory of Music. One day while walking with a friend in Atlanta, he pointed to a home he had never seen before, and predicted, "Do you see that house on the hill? A princess lives there. I am going to marry her."

A short time later one of his students introduced him to Ann Ree, who was asked to help the foreign-born musician improve his English. When Alexander took her home, he was surprised to learn that she lived in the "house on the hill." The two continued to see each other, and were married on April 16, 1916. One year later their daughter, Harriette Valaria, was born.

In the interval between her seventeenth year and twentieth year, the manifestations of Ann Ree's spiritual powers were more widely spaced, for she was absorbed by the changes in her life which had moved her so quickly from a young girl to the responsibilities of a wife and mother.

During the time of the great Atlanta fire Ann Ree was visiting her parents. As she stood with her father, daughter, and husband, watching the raging flames, all were startled and frightened when they heard "a great voice" call Ann Ree's name three times. Shortly after this significant event, a strong clairvoyance returned to her, and there was a guidance which had within it a more definite trend toward perfecting the use of her spiritual powers.

In her twenty-first year, while living in New York City, Ann Ree overcame an unpleasant occurrence which had disturbed her since early childhood. Whenever she had had a fever, a decaying old visage would appear at the foot of her bed and murmur in a monotone beat, "You are not sick." She later learned that this experience was part of a feeling of guilt or shame she unconsciously associated with sickness or ill health—a feeling she had brought into this life from former lives. When she overcame this feeling of guilt, she learned of the importance of certain fevers in a person's life, especially in the lives of children. She also learned that a fever produces an inverted rhythm in the blood which often attunes a person to the apparitional pictures in the lesser regions of the astral world—the little-known world between the physical world and the Spiritual Worlds.

It was in the period of her twenty-first year that Ann Ree began to witness certain obnoxious phenomena. Spoons, knives and other objects would raise themselves from the kitchen table and "just float around." She refused to be interested in this phenomenon and would have nothing to do with it. These levitation pranks continued until one day she said, "Stop!" Her intuition that such phenomena were of an unhealthy origin was later confirmed as being correct, for she learned that experiences with phenomena constitute a dangerous period in every initiate's life—a period in which the satanic forces tempt the initiate to enter the path of exploitation and black magic.

In a spiritual life one comes to innumerable crossroads—and the crossroad where black magic is presented is one of the most glamorous of all. No one can be trapped into the path of occult magic unless he inwardly desires to gain without earning. Persons who are caught in the snare of psychical phenomena become static in their evolvement.

The initiate must choose between the path of magic and the path of the spiritual life. Thus he must first learn the difference between magic and miracles. This is one of the finest points of all.

Immediately following my experiences and tests with the phenomena, my second daughter was conceived, and I began to have another level of spiritual association with the Inner Worlds. I was aware of the karmic nuances and the grace of the one preparing for birth through my body. I was also aware of the angels' help.

This pregnancy was connected with a deep introspection mirrored through nostalgic, spiritual moods. One evening I was aware of a complete fusion between the soul to be born and my own soul. I was then seven months pregnant.

It has always been my grace to have around me those who are not bound by formal religions, and in my marriage I had the encouragement of my husband to develop my intellectual and spiritual capacities. During my second pregnancy I did much research in various libraries, and I began to identify the powers working through me since childhood. Until this time I had no name for these powers; I had not associated with anyone who had such powers, nor did I feel any compulsion to search out persons in the world to interpret them.

There was a strong conviction within me to keep secret the continuing stream of inner experience; for an inner guidance convinced me that to share it with the unknowing would profane the very sacred part of my being, and what I knew to be real.

This attitude toward my spiritual gifts has remained with me all of my life: I must first prove *each thing to myself.*

The birth of my second child, Ann Ree II, brought me better spiritual alignment, a knowledge of the angelic worlds and, at last, the ability to speak with the etheric one who had directed my childhood visions. Our first audible meeting occurred while I was nursing my infant daughter at my breast. The first thing I noticed were his eyes, and I recognized them to be the same magnificent eyes seen by me since early childhood. As he stood before me, he was surrounded by a pulsating, filigreed medallion of white light. He did not speak his name, but I knew him to be the one called Master Morya. He said, "I have been with you a long time." The full significance of his statement was not wholly clear to me, for I had no conception then of re-embodiment. I was later to learn that he meant he had known me through many lives.

In this first audible meeting Master Morya told me, "You were — — before. You lived in England." A short time later I was to experience for myself the proof of my having lived this former life in England. It occurred in the following manner:

One evening while yet awake, I released my body and found myself in a room in which the walls and ceiling of heavy stone exuded a cold moisture. I was suspended at a height, looking down upon a burial bier with two candles at each end. A woman's body was being prepared for burial. Her long auburn hair touch-

ing the floor held my attention. On looking closely at the features they appeared to be my own—and I was aware it was I in another time. A large woman standing at the head of the bier was arranging the hair. Her back being turned to me, I was only able to determine that she was a maid-servant who lovingly ministered to her mistress in this time of death. By the maid's apparel, I saw the time or period to be the seventeenth century, and I knew the country to be England.

I experienced the extension and conclusion of this scene over twenty years later. I had just returned home from the hospital after a serious illness. A close friend and student, who was attending me as a nurse, went to the window to push back the heavy curtains. With this gesture the room was immediately transformed, becoming the room of another time—and I recognized this student as the woman at the head of the bier in the cold chamber of death.

In her twenty-fourth year Ann Ree began to receive telepathic, philosophical instruction from Master Morya, or Master M. His telepathy inspired her to write in a philosophic and poetic vein and to paint symbolic scenes. Her first oil paintings included a series of Higher-World scenes titled "The White Temples." These paintings were accompanied by poetic thoughts.

Think on pure, white temples,
On hallowed halls,
On far off musics,
On far off calls—
Nearing, nearer,
Clearing, clearer.
And thou thinkest on God.

The "white temples" are the Hall of Learning in the First Heaven. In the Hall of Learning the initiate crosses the threshold into the mysteries of Heaven. The majority of the initiate's experiences in the Hall of Learning occur during sleep. However, each initiatory experience of the night invariably correlates to some action in the waking state.

All who enter into the Hall of Learning come under the direction of the Cherubim Angels, the custodians of the symbolic codes of the First Heaven. The freshet poems *received by the initiate are under the direction of the Cherubim Angels. Music, poetry, and art are made more profound when one is instructed by the Cherubim Angels.*

One night while Ann Ree was resting alone on her bed, three Masters appeared by the side of the bed and looked directly at her. She was startled by the directness of their gaze and the dazzling colors in their bodies of light. To shield her eyes from the brilliance of their combined light, she pulled the bed covers over her eyes, but the covers would not dim or shut out the bright light that blazed through the room. This was the first time that more than one Master had appeared at the same moment. The three Masters who appeared by her bedside were Master M, Master K. H. and Master Hilarion. After this experience Ann Ree noticed an increase of telepathic power in painting and writing.

Later in her life Ann Ree learned that there are seven Masters who work telepathically with the advanced disciple-initiates of the earth. She learned that the Masters are part of a network or medallion of mediators who work to unite men with the Sovereign Mediator, the Lord Jesus.

Over the years she became familiar with the symbols and etheric appearance of each Master. She learned that six Masters dwell in the Second Heaven, or Spheres of Light—and that Master G. Q., the one Master remaining on earth, will leave the world at the end of the twentieth century. When the six Masters lived on earth they contributed to the spiritual and philosophical cultures of the world through lives of greatness. Several of the past lives of the Masters were revealed to her so that she could better understand the specific work of each Master and its influence upon the minds and souls of men in the present age. She often referred to the Masters as "the Great Immortals."

One day in her twenty-fourth year, when Ann Ree was painfully ill with quinsy, Master M appeared to her and said, "'Many are called, but few are chosen.' Thou art chosen. The way will be hard. Thou wilt lose everything to gain everything."

When the Master told me that I was to lose everything to gain everything, I was young, naive, and green. I had no conception of what lay before me. Over the years I was to remember his words. No matter how hard I tried to regulate my life to the timing of permanent relationships, my visions and revelations were my only permanency and security.

After I came under the instruction of the Master, I lived in a constant state of spiritual preparation. While I met my human responsibilities, my thoughts were constantly occupied with themes of instruction for some distant persons as yet unknown to me. I was

Ann Ree, age 12.

Age 16.

Ann Ree (far right) age 15, with relatives.

Ann Ree with daughter Harriette, August 7, 1917.

In Boston, 1921.

Ann Ree (right) with daughters Harriette (center) and Ann Ree II, 1938.

With five of her fourteen grandchildren, 1947.

Barjona, 1953. Ann Ree Colton and Jonathan Murro stand beside two of their paintings, "The Ascended Jesus" (left) and "Raphael Rain."

Pasadena, California, 1955.

convinced inwardly that in the near future I would meet these kindred persons who would accept what I had to say.

Master M instructed Ann Ree (who was naturally right-handed) to paint for six months with her left hand. He explained that this would help to overcome the harsh psychical and sub-electrical currents within the brain, so that she could begin to tap the grace-creative levels of her soul. Through her training with the Master she learned that, "All color in art retains the ether of the painter. The idea within the subject matter of the painting is imprinted upon the eye and mind of the beholder when the painting is produced through a spiritual rather than an egotistical impulse. When great paintings are consummated, the painter has united with his spiritual self; thus the works of an anointed artist become lasting portrayals, and men revere them."

Each night as I put my younger child to sleep, I saw around her crib the four Guardian Angels of the Cradle. When I saw my child in the angels' care, I felt free to take up my work of painting and writing under the direction of the Master.

One can identify a higher Being by the formation of light from his etheric body. If a Being has inhabited a physical body on earth, he emanates a medallion of filigreed light around *his etheric body. If the Being is an angel, thin lines of brilliant light emanate from* within *his body rather than from without.*

In her twenty-fourth year Ann Ree began to meditate each day under the telepathic direction of Master M; her painting time was limited by him to twice a week. During a meditation period she was told, "Wise have ye been to earn wisdom; but if ye would keep pure the gift of prophecy, ye must ask for understanding."

The Master instructed her to speak aloud a few extemporaneous words after her meditation each day. He explained that this practice was the means of sending into the world what she had experienced in meditation. As the years passed, her daily practice of extemporaneous speaking enabled her to perfect the spiritual gift of *telepathic logos.*

After my younger daughter's birth, I began to be overdirected and guided in a certain phase of evolvement in which I was trained by the Master to release my body for night-flight during sleep, and also for flight in the daytime while awake and in full consciousness. This training, which continued for seven years, enabled me to move safely over the abyss, or the lower regions of the astral world.

I always had a "consciousness" gift—that is, I did not use trance or any subjective means of separation from the outer consciousness. It was taught to me early by the Master that hypnosis in any form, self-induced or by another, is a violation of the will, and interferes with the Holy Ghost or direct receiving from the Spiritual Worlds.

I was given names, addresses of things yet to be (even thirty-three years distant in my life) and locations where my spiritual work was to be established in the future. The Master always spoke of my serving as "the work."

For two years I was trained in astrology and astronomy during my etheric flights before sleep. In a massive room with a small balcony, the Master showed me the zodiac of the earth and the zodiac of the heavens. Through this training I was later able to help many dedicated astrologers to research the deeper realities in astrology. The room with the balcony I later knew to be one portion of the Hall of Wisdom in the Spheres of Light, or Second Heaven.

In the beginning of my etheric flights, I saw cities laid out before me as in drawings or paintings. After a period of six months, the cities were no longer seen in this manner. They became places of reality, and I was able to touch the stones of buildings and to record their solidity through my etheric hands. Night after night I would release myself from my physical body before sleep, and fly in full consciousness over the continents and cities of the earth, noting many landmarks of historical importance. My hands touched the rooftops and window ledges of prominent buildings in these cities. I would enter into the buildings and absorb them into my memory and mind. Sometimes I examined the sacred tombs of saints, and touched the ancient, sacred relics of holy persons who had been martyred for their belief in God.

An Egyptian initiation phase also began in my etheric-flight experiences. This was to extend over a period of five years. My etheric flights into distant cities and buildings would invariably end in an ancient pyramid beneath the earth. At first, it would be very dark at the entrance to the pyramid, and I experienced a feeling of unseen danger. When I would say, "I am not afraid," the corridor would instantly light up and a Master would appear. Holding me by the hand, he would take me to the various chambers in the pyramid, and instruct me as to the hieroglyphics on the walls. I also received training in the reading of hieroglyphics inscribed on various tablets.

Even as I touched the buildings of cities with my etheric hands, so did I touch the hieroglyphics on the walls and on the tablets. The hieroglyphics were touched, felt, and then absorbed through my hands, imprinted upon my memory, and sealed into the etheric sheaths of my brain. On the following day I transcribed the hieroglyphics onto paper, and reinterpreted their disciplines and lessons.

Through these Egyptian initiatory experiences I recalled the old Atlantean and early Egyptian initiatory formulas that I had used in former lives. Throughout the years I have drawn upon these initiatory formulas, and have had access to their constant inner flow of meaning and wisdom. These symbologies and ritual formulas have aided me through many degrees and phases of revelation.

There was one chamber in the pyramid in which I was taught about embalming and the secrets of the dead, and of the profane priests of the dead. I was shown that some of these profane priests have reincarnated in the present age, and may be found in many walks of life. Such persons are dangerous to the world, for they have cunning, psychical knowledge of the subtle worlds, particularly concerning the power of the sub-elementals who are willing servants of those who use the dark or magical powers.

My instruction as to the secrets of death, and life after death, disclosed to me the true death ritual, which enables the dead to rise above the earthbound state.

In the pyramid I was initiated into the laws and judgments; I learned of the law of God's equation and of eternity justice, or karma. I was taught that man's conscience is an instrument of his soul. I was shown how the soul refuses to give rest to the mind until balance has been made between right and wrong. I learned that there are great laws in command of the earth, and that he who would ignore them or deny them destroys himself. I was shown that there are some in the world who know more about these laws than others do, and that it is their responsibility to teach and to lead those who know less.

I was being slowly prepared for a great change to come in my life, for within a period of eight years I was to be alone in the world.

Ann Ree's experiences in the pyramid also included the serpent or will initiations. She learned the importance of self-control and the use of the royal will, or the will immersed in the One or God. In the serpent initiations she was taught the formulas for higher levitation, or the release of her higher etheric body into night-flight; she learned how to rise etherically over the gravity currents of the earth. While receiving the formulas for higher levitation, she learned of manifestation and de-manifestation. This gave her the power to translate the lower degrees of ether into higher degrees of light. She also acquired the techniques of *etheric visitation,* which enabled her to make her etheric presence visible to others.

In the serpent initiations, certain portals in her brain were opened so that she could retain the memory of dreams and interpret them. Her soul's medallion was activated so that she could recollect and research her past lives, and thus be prepared in the coming years to unveil the past lives of others. She was taught how to send her thoughts and how to manifest healing at a distance. She was given the power to insulate herself from the dangers of the dark, and she was shown how to sustain the equilibrium of her physical atoms, that she might receive longevity grace in her later years.

As she grew older, the inner initiatory formulas sealed into Ann Ree through the pyramid initiations manifested themselves one by one.

An Angel of Hope, the first angel to speak to Ann Ree, told her that his work was to help those who are mentally despondent.

The Angels of Hope work with both the living and the dead. If a person has acquired the attribute of mercy, his grace enables the Angels of Hope to come to him, to lift his thoughts, and to help him rise over the pitfalls of self-reproach and melancholy.

After her experience with the Angel of Hope, the Cherubim Angels began to show Ann Ree how she would use her prophetic gifts in the coming years. She was repeatedly cautioned by the Cherubim Angels that prophecy could be used as an instrument for fear rather than for good. She was told that to give personal prophecy out of timing would invoke the spirit of revenge. Over the years she learned to define the difference between the psychical and the spiritual levels of prophecy. She also discerned that there are "predictive possibles and prophetic certainties."

As the years shaped me, I learned to determine the difference between a predictive possible and a prophetic certainty. A predictive possible *is influenced by the will of the one receiving the prophecy. If the person has the grace, his prayers and higher will can modify and sometimes divert a predictive possible containing a negative portent. When a predictive possible holds a promise for good, a person's belief and faith in the prophecy can precipitate good actions and events. A* prophetic certainty *is an ordained event which is inescapable, regardless of prayer or the human will.*

The Cherubim Angels gave Ann Ree long-range personal prophecies to show what her work would be in the world. These prophecies were in the form of poetry. In her twenty-fourth year she was told by the Cherubim: "Ye shall wear a golden gown, and ye shall know renown."

The Cherubim Angels taught me to recognize the telepathic code of warning and apprehension given through music. At unexpected times, songs irrelevant to my mood would enter into my thoughts. I learned that the titles of these songs, tunes, or jingles were used to identify coming events, or to alert me to circumstances and occurrences at a distance. The Cherubim telepathy through music is but one form of telepathic communication.

The Cherubim telepathy often contained verses of instruction. The following poem was written in her twenty-fourth year:

Did you do with good intent
Things accused?
Did you blindly, though well-meant,
Wrongly choose?
There is a Law protecting
The fool who falls,
And hinders not his rise again.
He who tries, will find his way once more.

Ann Ree was twenty-four years old when she started to research and identify the astral origin of certain diseases and sicknesses. Before her children contracted a contagious disease, such as scarlet fever, whooping cough, or measles, she was invariably prewarned through vision or direct clairvoyance. In full waking consciousness, she would go to the bacteria levels of the astral world, and study and examine the magnified germ, learning the origin and cause of the sickness, as well as how to care for her children. This gift of healing and supersensory diagnosis has continued throughout her life.

In the latter part of her twenty-fourth year Ann Ree began to make kabalistic paintings; while doing these paintings she heard Master M's voice instruct her in the cosmos and cosmic realities. The Master explained to her that the mathematics within kabala enabled her to overcome the psychic or astral currents and to make direct alignment with the Spiritual Worlds.

For a two-year period, books and other reading matter, with the exception of historical and biographical literature, were withheld from her so as not to color what she was receiving from the Master.

The kabalistic paintings continued into her early thirties, and united her with the cosmos and cosmic symbols of the universe. These paintings quickened the gift of *sacred nomenclature*—a spiritual gift which enabled her to discern the sacred or grace names of persons, and to name and identify the soul-meaning in the paintings or written freshets of others.

The kabalistic paintings were preparation for the time when she would undergo certain initiatory experiences with the symbologies of the Higher Worlds. These initiatory experiences would eventually qualify her to interpret the greater archetypes of the Third Heaven.

Before I reached my twenty-fifth year, my visions were beautiful, mystical, and spontaneous; however, I did not understand the full meaning of my visions and dreams until I began to paint kabalistically. When I began to paint the kabalistic story of creation, my spiritual powers became coordinated. Through these colorful, geometrical paintings, the downpouring of telepathic instruction was opened to me. Thereafter, the meaning within the deeper symbologies began to be revealed. Whenever I neglected to pray, meditate, or paint, the Spiritual Worlds and their great ideas were veiled from me.

In her twenty-fourth year Ann Ree was told by Master M that she would establish a church in Florida. In her twenty-fifth year she began to have visions of the peninsula of Florida surrounded by a rosy light, and she felt a nostalgic yearning to incorporate the State of Florida into her being. In her twenty-sixth year it was made possible for her to live in Florida.

During her first years in Florida she suffered many adversities and trials, due to the financial depression of the nation. Through direct experience she learned something of the hardships and temptations existing in the world. From these harsh lessons, between her twenty-ninth year and thirty-second year, she became more spiritually sensitive, and she also became a more practical disciple. Thus she was prepared for the challenges of the ministerial years ahead.

In the balmy Florida air I penetrated deeper levels of meditation. My kabalistic paintings and hieroglyphic writings continued. Though I was exposed to hardships in my outer life, my spiritual life never wavered.

It was my custom each day to meditate under the trees of my home. There was dense foliage and moist grass in the area where I meditated. One day I looked up to see I had a visitor accompanying my meditation; he was a large cottonmouth moccasin. His body was in a half upright position, swaying to the rhythm of my quiet. The serpent remained in this position during my complete meditation, and when I concluded my meditation, he moved harmlessly away. This experience with the water moccasin coincided with certain serpent initiatory rituals I had recently experienced through hieroglyphic instruction.

In my disciplines and training in Florida, Master M gave me a simple spiritual exercise to rejuvenate my lesser etheric body—the body of etheric vitality. I was directed to kneel with palms outstretched before me, and to say the words, "I set free the vital forces of my being." I was told to follow this sentence with any loving, creative words that would come into my mind. It was explained to me that this posture enabled the psychic brain within the solar plexus to be sealed away. I was particularly impressed to remember that the pressure on the knees during a spoken prayer is a vital necessity to open the spiritual portals around the heart.

My Florida home was surrounded by Australian pines. During these days of contemplation and meditation I heard the inner musics and sounds of Heaven as they moved with the wind through the trees. In this clean, pure environment I concluded a cycle in my spiritual life, for soon I would begin my ministry. My hours of contemplation and introspection would henceforth be spent in prayers for others.

In my first years in Florida I had certain reserve and strength because I remained under the continued instruction of Master M. This instruction from the Master was interrupted by the many demands that were placed upon me in my ministry. However, I was comforted by the knowledge that his thoughts, love, and blessings were with me. Even though I was no longer under his direct telepathic tutelage, I often met him in dreams—and in crisis times he appeared to me.

Ann Ree began her ministry in 1932. Her entry into the ministry came about in a surprising and unexpected manner. Her mother said to a friend in serious trouble, "Why don't you see my daughter? She knows how to look into people's troubles. And she will be able to help you."

Ann Ree was able to help the woman—and after this first interview, a steady stream of people sought her spiritual guidance and counsel. In the same year she assembled her first group and taught her first class.

Until this time my mother had been my inquisitor, scoffing at my religious beliefs and discounting my visions. Whatever was between my soul and my mother's soul was rectified when she opened the door for my future work.

Throughout my life I had lived in a continuing state of visions and in an awareness of God's World. No one needed to convert me to believe in God. I knew that God Is, *because I saw His World at all times.*

I am amazed when people do not believe in the angels, for I have always lived with the angels and their ministering helps.

My greatest suffering has come from agnostic persons.

Even though I received visions, I learned from my association with the Presences of Heaven that I was not exempt from human experience. I would make my mistakes and suffer, even as other persons in the world. I have seen it proved time and time again that my willful acts were not condoned by Heaven. The prophet is no exception. When a prophet willfully steps aside from the law of God, he suffers—and he takes upon himself the suffering of those he harms. However, I have also known that Heaven's help is given without stint whenever there is an urgent need for myself or for others.

Those who became a cross to me in my personal life, were removed from my life. Even though I would have humanly desired to sustain the relationships, such persons who put a stumbling block between me and my spiritual life were removed through uncontrollable cir-

cumstances. This I have counted as grace. As time went on, I became free of possessive persons. Only when I reached the period of equanimity as a prophet and server for God did I receive the blessing and harmony of perfect relationships.

In my thirty-third year I learned that there were persons who were anxious to learn from me what I knew of Heaven. From this time on, my prophetic powers were extended. I learned what every prophet comes to know—that through the exchange of spiritual conversation, the power of prophecy is increased.

I began my work during the depression of 1932. Many of the people who sought my help were suffering from hunger and were without promise of work of any sort. It was my grace to help them to enter into deeper levels of faith and to use degrees of courage they had never used. My prophetic insight proved to be a lamp for their feet.

The prophetic power of Ann Ree became a compass to direct persons to locations or to individuals holding the answers to their needs. Her insight also perceived certain hidden assets or skills within these persons that were unknown to themselves; thus, many who came to her for help changed to vocations that were more conducive to their souls' expressions.

3

The Miraculous Years

And God hath set some in the church, first apostles, secondarily prophets, thirdly teachers, after that miracles, then gifts of healing, helps, governments, diversities of tongues.

—I Corinthians 12:28

From her thirty-third year to her forty-ninth year, Ann Ree became well known for her spiritual gifts, especially for her ability to prophesy with accuracy. During these years she was visited by an endless chain of searching humanity from all strata of society. Among those who sought the wisdom of her counsel were prominent lawyers, doctors, inventors, bankers, ministers, governors.

Many desperate people came to her; many curiosity seekers came; many with faith also came. The latter remained to receive spiritual instruction. While serving thousands of persons, she gained a vast reservoir of knowledge about the human spirit, its needs, and its soul-aspirations.

In 1933 Ann Ree began a ten-year cycle in which her personal karma was to be laid aside, and while helping others she was to be protected spiritually to withstand the pressures of the world. She made a covenant with her Guardian Angel to serve people, realizing that when this ten-year period was over she would have to meet her personal karma. During this cycle she achieved prophetic excellence in her work in Florida, rendering a reverent service to persons in need—and those who became her students blended with her in perfect unison.

Ann Ree had the conviction that she must adhere to the timing of her weekly class, which began at eight o'clock each Thursday evening. Persons having plans of their own often tried to divert her from her obligation to her students, but she could not be diverted.

When the Governor's wife called from Tallahassee and asked for an appointment on Thursday night, she was told that Ann Ree would be teaching a class and would be unable to see her. Nevertheless, the Governor's wife came to Ann Ree's home and expected to see her. Ann Ree explained to her the spiritual importance of the class and that the many persons who came for instruction must not be disappointed. The Governor's wife agreed, and remained in the city overnight so that she could see her on the following day.

All true teachers of the spiritual sciences come to know that the currents of devotion are delicate and can be easily diverted. Ann Ree realized that if she had disrupted the weekly rhythm of her teaching tryst, her students would have lost step with the timing of their souls.

My more reverent and spiritually inclined students requested that we form a church. On November 1, 1936, a church was founded upon the first part of Corinthians, the twelfth chapter. Until this time people had come to my door and had partaken of spiritual bread, sometimes thinking it to be magical bread. From the time my church was founded, the public ceased to classify my work as occultism.

The little church was the natural step in the order of events, for around me were a number of persons who hungered, as I hungered, for a spiritual home.

When my church was formed, the psychical and occult persons around me did not respond to the devotional side of my work. It was then I began to realize that many persons who had taken up the occult life totally ignored the Bible and the need for devotional worship.

I continued my esoteric classes for those who were yet without religious affiliation. Gradually, many of these esoteric and occult persons developed their devotional natures and became part of the church.

In thousands of instances, whenever there was a legitimate need, Ann Ree proved to be helpful with her prophetic and healing gifts. Through numerous experiences of trial and error, she learned to give prophetic help prudently and wisely, so as not to interfere with a person's right to experience a lesson necessary for his soul-growth. In this training she developed the ability to know when to give and when to withhold prophetic information. She learned that persons who had offended prophetic laws in their former lives, even though they sought help and enlightenment in this life, would invariably misinterpret the "timing" of a prophecy. Although they received help, their souls demanded that they still experience the lessons concealed within their sorrows and problems.

The unbelieving of some—and, in others, a hidden conviction of self-guilt—prevented their benefiting from help given in time of crisis.

While Ann Ree's work had a spiritual background, there were those who did not interpret her gifts in a spiritual way, and sought her out only for material or personal gain. Because it was her conviction that she could not turn anyone away in the hour of need, such persons through the years gradually became an oppressive burden upon her.

One morning I awakened to find a woman at the foot of my bed. She said, "Are you Ann Ree Colton? You've got to help me." After this experience I employed a secretary so that I could retain a certain amount of privacy. Juanita Gledhill, a very competent secretary, remained with me for thirteen years; she was a woman of love, devotion and integrity. Juanita was an English woman who had strong Anglican Church beliefs. She had a delicious sense of humor, but was dignified and resourceful at all times.

Between the years of 1932 and 1945, every conceivable human problem was presented to me. During this period of time, my prophetic insight became like fine steel filed to hypersensitivity. When a stranger crossed the threshold of my study, I knew him instantly. Before a word was spoken, I knew his weaknesses and his strengths, his problems and his motivations—and I knew his reason for coming to me.

The gleaming brain, called the "third eye" by some, had become so sensitive that I experienced for many days at a time the sensation of wearing a small crown on the apex of my head.

I realized that when people brought me their personal problems there was a way to bring them closer to their souls, and, in this, I had help from the angelic worlds. But when persons brought me materialistic or money problems I was always in danger from a psychic world—and this was a constant strain.

When some came to me interested only in materialistic affairs, it was solely dependent upon the grace of the individual whether he could be aided, and his level of purity determined the degree to which he could be helped.

I learned that I could not sit in judgment on others, nor could I use discrimination concerning persons who sought me out, but that such selection must be made by a work "behind the scenes"—that is, the spiritual, mediative help of Heaven. So it was increasingly necessary that I myself remain in a spiritual state without judgments, and remain very close to the Bible as the origin of true prophecy.

A physician, living in the northern part of Florida, who was known for his specialized psychological and psychiatric work with alcoholics, became himself addicted to drink. He was a student of the esoteric philosophies and sought out Ann Ree for help. During his particularly difficult times he would telephone her late in the evening, and say he was on his way to see her, arriving at two-thirty or three o'clock in the morning. After a series of approximately ten of these visits, the doctor was restored to his normal state, and the possessing entity he had attracted, which caused him to desire alcohol, removed itself.

Ann Ree was shown that in a previous life this man

had been a lama wearing a yellow robe in Tibet. She saw that in this austere life he had failed to restrain his senses, and that his senses still bore the mark of gluttony. This made it possible for him to be entity-possessed, and thus subjected to desire for alcohol.

A prominent clubwoman, the wife of a doctor, came to Ann Ree in desperation. The woman had become an habitual drinker, and her husband had almost reached the limit of his patience with her. On leaving Ann Ree one afternoon, the woman began to drink and continued until she became unconscious. She awakened early the next morning with the feeling of disaster. Going into her husband's room, she found that he had removed all of his possessions and had indeed left her. Suddenly, Ann Ree appeared in her etheric body and said to the woman, "Everything will be all right at three o'clock this afternoon."

The woman's husband returned home at three o'clock. Her experience with Ann Ree frightened and impressed the woman, and thereafter she refrained from drinking.

The prayers and guidance of Ann Ree were effective in the healing of a number of persons addicted to alcohol. Often, frantic persons would ask healing for alcoholic mates. In many instances such persons would return to Ann Ree to thank her for the miracle of healing which had transformed their marriages.

Indeed, Ann Ree's spiritual helps were channeled in many unexpected ways, and fulfilled many pressing needs.

A young girl, a member of Ann Ree's church, was riding with a boy friend who sought to force the girl into sexual intimacy. Ann Ree, using the power of etheric visitation, appeared in the automobile with the girl and the boy. The boy, seeing the new passenger, was diverted from his ideas of seduction and escorted the girl safely home.

A woman, who held a prominent position in an organization dealing with afflicted children, became interested in Ann Ree's paintings and counseling help. The woman's eighteen-year-old daughter, deaf and mute since birth, was attracted to Ann Ree and would often visit her. One day the daughter startled her mother when she began to hear and speak. Rather than thanking God for this miraculous manifestation of healing, the mother became frustrated and disturbed, for she feared that her place of prominence in the organization for afflicted children would be jeopardized. In her confusion the woman asked Ann Ree, "What will I do with my life now?" The woman was also embittered because she did not know how to explain to others the way in which her daughter was healed.

In her ministry Ann Ree was especially able to help the pure in heart. Children always responded to her healing prayers, and in some instances the healings were miraculous.

A medical doctor, who had conscientiously and honestly practiced medicine for many years, became interested in the occult sciences. Unfortunately, he affiliated himself with an unethical occult school. In his occult practices, the doctor prematurely opened certain psychic portals within his solar plexus and at the base of his skull. Having no religious background or beliefs, he was unable to differentiate between the psychical and the spiritual, and he felt himself to be under the direction of a Master, when in reality he had become a victim of a subtle *astral guru*.

When this doctor came to Ann Ree, she saw that he had fallen into the "ore snare"—which is so common in subversive occult acts. Under the direction of the astral guru, he had begun to sink oil wells, only to find sand, sulphur, shell, and water. His obsession to find oil in Florida had caused him to draw upon the financial resources of his friends and others. Because he was essentially an honest man, he was conscience-stricken, and passed night after night in sleeplessness. Ann Ree disclosed to the doctor that he was under the influence of psychic hypnosis. However, the doctor was unable to receive a healing because he refused to have the entity he called his "master" exorcised. Being too enmeshed in the psychic coil, he could not escape; shortly thereafter he took his life.

In her research Ann Ree found that the greater number of persons who take their lives are under entity-control, and that such persons are not wholly responsible for the act of suicide.

One way I was able to determine whether a person was under the influence of an astral guru was by the appearance of the skin on the face and the hands. One who has given himself to entity possession has a waxen pallor to the skin. The face appears bloated, and there is usually an unhealthy moisture on the face and the palms of the hands. The face of an entity-possessed person becomes corpse-like with yellowish or bruised tinges beneath the eyes. The eyes are evasive, refusing to look into the eyes of another person. In the case of this doctor, I saw the astral guru directing him, and I knew that in a former life the doctor had offended ethics as to wealth, honor, and possessions. Even though on the surface he was honest, he had yet retained cupidity from a former life, and thus was open to psychic hypnosis.

Before the second World War a wealthy industrialist often visited Ann Ree, and on several occasions he sent his chemists and engineers to her, so that she might aid them with their formulas and in the designing of machinery. The answers to some of their problems were close to their minds, but still veiled from them. Through her second sight and also her ability to draw on past-life knowledge of things mechanical, Ann Ree was able to perceive and articulate the answers sought by the chemists.

One day Ann Ree opened the door of her study and was surprised to see three persons with contrasting backgrounds conversing amiably on the subjects of religion and politics. One was a distinguished industrialist, another was a woman associate of a renowned woman evangelist, and the third was Emma, a prostitute.

Before Emma became a prostitute, she had been a maid for Ann Ree's invalid sister. Emma had been born with only two small fingers on her left hand, and she was forced to take menial work due to her handicap. She was a beautiful girl, well-educated, and had been reared in a strict religious family. In her twenty-third year Emma became involved with an amoral man; she left the service of Ann Ree's sister and became a prostitute.

Four years later Emma came to Ann Ree for help, because she longed to escape from her unhappy life. Through the spiritual influence of Ann Ree, Emma and her companion prostitutes were able to walk out on the madam who had exploited them. Shortly thereafter, Emma received a token of grace. A man, who had lost his arm in an accident, fell in love with her, and for the first time in her life the afflicted girl knew happiness.

After Emma and the other girls had packed their bags and returned to their homes, the madam called on Ann Ree and asked, "You told the girls to leave me, didn't you?" Ann Ree answered, "I did." The madam said, "I thought you did." Thereafter the madam was unable to re-establish her activities in the city.

When a diamond bracelet worth thousands of dollars was lost, the owner consulted Ann Ree, who instantly saw in a vision the exact location of the missing bracelet. The owner followed her directions and found the bracelet in the place indicated by the vision.

A little boy was heartbroken after his shetland pony strayed away. The boy's grandmother, who had given him the pony, asked Ann Ree for help. Ann Ree drew a map for the grandmother, and explained how to find the pony. When the pony was found in the place described, the little boy was overjoyed. Then he paused and reflected on *how* his pony was recovered. Turning to his grandmother, he asked, "Grandmother, what *is* Ann Ree?"

A woman forgot where she had hidden some money and called on Ann Ree to help locate it. Even though Ann Ree had never before seen the woman, she said to her, "You live in a one-and-a-half story house. Go upstairs into a room where you have a chest of drawers. In the third drawer down, look under some young boy's clothes and you will find the money. These were the clothes of your ten-year-old boy who is dead." The woman found the money in the drawer containing the clothes of her young son who had passed away.

The recovery of the money turned out to be of secondary importance to the woman, for she felt in her heart that her son had helped in recovering the money, thereby proving to her that he still lived after death. Due to this experience the mother's grief for her son was assuaged.

When a small boy was lost in a snow storm in the mountains of California, the parents contacted Ann Ree. She told them that their son was with another lad, and at that moment the boys were safely approaching a Ranger station. A short time later the parents were notified by the Rangers that their son and his companion had been found.

A child living in England pierced her eye with a thorn while stooping over a rose bush. The surgeon who examined the eye said that the eye must be removed "within the fortnight." The mother of the child, being associated with one of Ann Ree's students in the United States, cabled the student to ask for Ann Ree's help. When the child was brought to the surgeon for the operation, a second examination disclosed no need for surgery, for the eye was completely healed.

The healing power working through Ann Ree was especially effective when persons requested healing for eye afflictions. It was later revealed to her that she had earned this gift in a former life in which she had suffered blindness. This revelation gave her the clue as to why some healers are more proficient in the healing of certain types of afflictions or diseases. She learned that when one has mastered a sickness through absolute faith, he earns the grace of healing power for that particular sickness. She also learned that when men have obtained a spiritual immunity from the twelve bacterial levels causing sickness in the world, they will have the power to give perfect health to others, even as did the Lord Jesus who healed all manners of diseases.

During the war many women who had sons and husbands in the service sought Ann Ree's help. One distressed woman who came to her about a soldier-son reported missing in action was comforted when Ann Ree told her that her son was alive and a prisoner. In a vision Ann Ree saw the son being transported to Germany in a boxcar. She told the mother that her son had been wounded, and described his wound. She also gave the date of his return. Everything she told the mother about her son proved to be correct.

Soon after World War II was over, a man and wife who had studied the esoteric and occult sciences, and who had heard about Ann Ree's spiritual powers, came from Pennsylvania to see her. The woman was in a state of distress. Previous to her present marriage, she had been married to a soldier who had been reported killed in action; however, due to continued dreams of her former husband, the woman was convinced that he was still living. Ann Ree told the couple that the man was alive and that he was living in Tennessee. She named the small town in Tennessee where he was living and drew a map describing the location and appearance of his house. She told the couple that they would find him coming around the side of the house with a hoe on his shoulder.

It was later reported to Ann Ree that the meeting took place exactly as predicted. After the first greetings were over, the man told the couple that when he learned he had been reported dead, he decided to live another life, a life of simplicity. He raised no obstacle to a divorce so that the couple might be remarried.

A lawyer came to Ann Ree about a client who was facing the death penalty. She told the lawyer that if he would have the trial postponed until a certain date, his client's life would be spared. The lawyer followed her advice, and his client was sentenced to life imprisonment rather than to the electric chair.

Time after time, the validity of her gifts was proven in matters of both minor and major importance. However, her spiritual powers would not function for unscrupulous or dishonest persons.

During her years of close association with the public, her powers were brought into a sharp focus, and she gained an invaluable insight into the diverse levels of human expression.

It was not necessary for Ann Ree to be in the physical proximity of one who requested help. Whenever she was contacted by mail or telephone, she could see into the souls of those seeking help, regardless of the distance.

No matter where I was—on the street or on the telephone—the prophetic power automatically began to function whenever a person asked me a question.

Some people took advantage of this, and even when I went into public places, such as restaurants, there was no privacy. Their intrusions disturbed my peace and devitalized me.

The walls of Ann Ree's study were lined with books which she personally bought to give (as one of her ways of tithing) to those who indicated that they were ready to answer and put to use the persistent prompting of their souls' grace. In this, she extended her instruction by giving them a physical symbol—books—that they might begin to seek their own solutions to their problems, and thereby receive self-help and guidance.

When a person in sorrow or need seeks the answer through a human teacher or counselor, this is always in obedience to his soul's prompting; the wise teacher hands the person the means by which he may find himself, and thus experience the privilege of self-discovery. While the teacher's work is to reveal certain threads in one's unresolved soul-debts and in his potential soul-grace—often through a needed and extended instruction—there is always the time when the one seeking help must deal directly with the world within himself, wherein lies the true solution to his problems.

Ann Ree knew this cardinal law: prophetic counseling must be accompanied by instruction. To reveal knowledge to anyone at unrest in his life-pattern, without giving instruction, is to place a burden or responsibility upon the teacher. When instruction is absent, the teacher takes upon himself the karma of the one seeking help, thus preventing the person from experiencing the rewards of self-revealing and self-knowing. The spiritual teacher must recognize the right time to give knowledge and instruction, and must also know the time for silence. When the teacher realizes that a student is unready for certain instruction, the Higher Worlds inspire the teacher to release the student to the level of mediation holding the answer to the student's need and evolvement. Because of this method and technique in Ann Ree's work, those seeking sensation through psychic phenomena rarely came to more than one interview or attended more than three classes.

During my ministry I learned that among all races there are some persons who have a strongly rooted desire for psychic phenomena and for practices of elemental magics. This type of person invariably fell away from that which I taught, for they were unable to devote themselves to the spiritual practices placed before them as a means of escape from a decadent psychic coil.

There are many in the world today in varied walks of life who retain a psychic, atavistic memory; such persons desire to use remembered inverted practices in Nature. These are a laggard remnant from Atlantean and early Egyptian days who failed to follow the remembered Light. From age to age they hold only to the practices of powers retained through self-will. Therefore, in the present life, they feel compelled to use the same magical powers, or are attracted to those who possess them. While a certain element of faith is used in these powers, such inverted practices violate both faith and power.

Those who seek to exert their selfish wills over others or to gain possessions without earning them, abuse both faith and power, and open the door for base psychic magic. But those who follow the Lord Jesus in the use of love and light are able, through the help of the angels, to overcome such insidious powers which are detrimental to the pure will of man.

A small percentage of persons who received Ann Ree's counseling help became students. Some of her most highly evolved students had sought her out at first to help them with commonplace problems; some were desperate and called on her when all else had failed, thinking their problem was material when, in reality, it was spiritual.

One such student wrote the following:

> June 2nd, 1938!—the day that changed my whole life. That was the day I met you—Ann Ree Colton.
>
> That day, when I first saw you, I thought, or I should say, I *felt,* I had known you before. There was something about your eyes, or rather there seemed to be a closed door in back of them just about to open.
>
> You knew I was searching. You were very patient with me that day in spite of my rudeness. You asked me if I had ever been to your church, and I said to you, "No, and I wasn't going either."
>
> I was horrified when you told me I had created the condition in which I found myself. How had I, when I had nothing to do with it? Mother had married the man, not I. I felt she wanted to have her cake (me) and eat it too (him). Yet I felt there was a chain around my neck and ankles, and according to you I had

put them there, no one else. I thought you were a bright woman, but you didn't know what you were talking about. You talked a long time and when I was leaving you said, "Please come and see me again, won't you? And have you changed your mind about coming to my church?" I said, "No, I haven't, but I'll think about it." And you said, "Well, you are honest." So I left, utterly bewildered and confused.

June 2nd was on Thursday. All that week your face was before me, especially your eyes. I couldn't think of anything but what you said. Your words seemed to be fire and burned into my mind.

We all three went to your church that night. I don't remember the topic of the sermon, but as you talked, there were flashes of light, one after another, in my mind, and I knew I had found what I had been looking for in Religion. I knew you had something no one else had. But what was it? You came down and stood in front of me and smiled and said, "You came; I am glad to see you."

As you know I found my Teacher, and haven't missed many of your church meetings since. The night you announced you were having classes I was in my glory. Here I was going to find out the meaning of karma, re-embodiment, consciousness, etc.

I went through many private hells when I did find out. My ego was being deflated, and, being a Scorpio, I didn't appreciate it very much. But, as you know, I came through when I found out "Man's extremity was God's opportunity," and I was willing to give God a chance; for surely I had made a mess of my way of thinking, acting and living.

You have been so patient with me through my stumbling, my stubbornness. I had many wonderful hours with you in your garden and many discussions took place; most of it was over my head, but I listened and stored it away for future use.

My garden is a thing of beauty. It has been the place of my regeneration. In my garden I can think and try to place the truths you taught me to the place where they belonged—within myself! And although it has taken many lessons to come even to this point, at least I am this far.

You have said how much better fresh vegetables tasted when love was growing them. Yes, I know now what you meant about growing a garden with love, and by loving my seeds and plants they absorbed the love through my hands and came to their fullest expression.

That was a new slant on love. Love, to me, was physical—and your teachings were of a spiritual love. Where was the difference? It didn't take me so very long to find out. I had better understanding after one of your talks on sex. Until that time sex was something ugly and repulsive to me and something in my mind which had nothing to do with love, not as I knew love. How could I ever understand the love between a man and a woman? I couldn't, for to me, that only meant sexual expression. As a nurse I had seen so many homes wrecked and children sitting around with frightened hearts listening to their parents fighting and quarreling, yet their parents had loved each other when they were married, or at least they were supposed to love one another. So, what was wrong? What was the answer?

Remember, I had lived all of my young womanhood years in homes where there were sick children or a sick mother, or a mother disgusted with marriage, yet bringing in another unwanted child. No wonder I had hate in my young mind half the time. The whole world was as ignorant as I was, and truly the whole world needs to have a reverent attitude toward sex.

*

I don't know how I could have gone on with such a tormented mind. Even though deep within my heart I knew you were telling me the truth, there was ever the constant fight between Spirit and physical. I am glad to say Spirit has won. You must have been sad at times watching that conflict. You knew you were right; you always were—and yet I deliberately went against you, trying to save my pride. I am glad to say there is no more of that kind of pride.

* * *

My dearly beloved Teacher,

This past summer has been a milestone in my life; you know of the severe test I went through.

Even though I was condemned to die by the doctor, I kept remembering that you said, "No one goes out until he has learned the lessons for which he came." I knew I was not ready to leave this body; I did not know enough. In fact, I did not know anything. By this time I had faith in you, your teaching, and firstly faith in the God who created me—faith to know He put me where I was, in your care, to learn of Him as a God of love and not a God of punishment to condemn me to such wracking pain without a reason. What was the reason?

Karma is certainly the answer to many questions. Re-embodiment is another—the answer to unhappy marriages, why children are born into such families. It pays to watch the things one does and says, for truly he pays and pays until the debt is replaced by the good he creates.

I know now that is how one grows, for how can one know good unless he knows evil? How can one grow unless he stumbles and falls? After each fall or each trial I know he is stronger than before. I think sometimes I am too weak to even make another try, but I have never shirked a duty, even a negative one; so I pick myself up and start all over again.

* * *

My beloved Teacher,

I visited your home today and you were ill again. You had been ill several times lately. Today you told me you might have to go to the hospital for an operation. I was deeply grieved to hear this, so I prayed and put you lovingly in the hands of the Father. Even though I knew the condition was serious, I knew in my heart you were needed here to carry on your great work and you would not pass on.

You said, "I know and feel a great change is taking place; I will either leave this body or become a better teacher." It is hard to realize you could be a better Teacher, for to me you are a great Teacher.

The people have flocked to your door and taken of your substance, and yet they do not realize what you are or what you have given them. One thing I do know, they asked for "bread" and were not given "a stone."

You teach that we are all spiritual beings in the making. It has taken so long to realize and absorb that great truth. How can we fail in anything if we let God use His Will?

* * *

My beloved Teacher and Friend,

Tomorrow you are being operated on. I asked you if I could go to the hospital and be with you. You said that I could stay with you.

Thank God, you are coming along fine now. I stayed with you until four-thirty that afternoon, and though you were very sick, I knew our prayers had been heard and answered.

On the tenth day the doctor said you could go home. Then you asked me if I would be able to take care of you. Nothing could have stood in my way, and my heart was full to overflowing with love and gratitude that I could do something for you.

*

In the two weeks I took care of you on your return from the hospital I learned many, many lessons.

You had a vision which showed you that we had been together in England in another embodiment; I had served you and your children. In the vision you saw yourself laid out in death and me pushing back the curtains to let in the morning light. You said, "I have wondered why you were so devoted to me; now I know."

That brought on a discussion of life after death and re-embodiment, and that we had lived many lives. This was one of the hardest ideas for me to accept. After that morning I had more understanding on the subject.

The part I could not understand was how the soul could enter into the fetus, or embryo. Finally I realized one could not see Spirit any more than he could see the wind. He knew the wind was blowing, but he could not see it.

* * *

The above excerpts are from a diary of letters written by Alma Jones between the years 1938 and 1945. Ann Ree did not learn of this diary of letters until after Alma's death on January 14, 1952. Alma Jones remained a loyal and devoted student until the day of her death.

When I met Alma Jones, she was forty-nine years of age, and she had lived a life of hardship and servi-

tude. Outwardly, she was a strong-willed, aggressive and competent woman; inwardly, she was a combination of timidity and seething resentment. The possessive attachment toward her mother prevented her freedom of action, and failing to respond to her soul's continued prompting, Alma became an embittered and sour personality. When her mother remarried, this placed Alma in the position of an unwelcome third in a triangle. Her stepfather loved his whiskey and kept their home in a state of constant tumult. When Alma Jones came under my instruction, the home life of these three people began to change. The stepfather was healed of drinking, and gradually the triangle became a triad of harmony.

In the latter part of her life, Alma Jones responded to her soul. She never ceased in her charitable good. Having a fine mind, she was able to help many others to perceive the life of the soul. Her faith and amazing vitality enabled her to overcome three major sicknesses diagnosed as fatal by physicians.

An elderly woman of rare soul-grace, called "Aunt Mary" by her friends, was another of Ann Ree's devoted students. In her eighty-sixth year Aunt Mary suffered a fractured ankle; a short time later she lost a dear son, who had been a writer of scenarios for a popular radio program. After the death of her son, Aunt Mary was left almost destitute. One night her son appeared to her in a dream and reminded her of a suitcase filled with his manuscripts. Aunt Mary immediately made contact with the sponsors of the radio program—who were delighted to purchase the manuscripts. The suitcase of manuscripts proved to be an *after-death will,* for Aunt Mary was thereafter free from financial worry. She called this providence her "pennies from Heaven."

Ann Ree was teaching from her altar at the moment of Aunt Mary's death. She knew that her beloved student had expired, for Aunt Mary appeared in her etheric body. With her quaint smile and depth of humor, Aunt Mary raised one finger of her hand—upon which was the papal ring. Ann Ree saw that Aunt Mary, in her next life, would become a pope of Rome, and as pope she would be responsible for the belief in palingenesis, or reincarnation, returning to the Catholic Church.

Persons hearing Ann Ree teach would often comment on her beautiful voice. One woman who was new to inspirational instruction said to her, "I cannot understand what you mean; I come just to hear your voice." Those who remarked about her lovely voice would have been surprised to learn that Ann Ree had been born with a slight speech impediment. This defect was overcome during the "logos" or speech training she received from the Master.

One Sunday, Ann Ree was surprised to see her mother sitting in the overflowing congregation. This was the first time her mother had come to hear her speak in public. During the sermon her mother remembered the days of Ann Ree's childhood when she taught the Bible to playmates. After the service her mother said, "Well, at last you are where you wanted to be."

The following article, titled "Recollection on Mother's Day," was written by Ann Ree for her church magazine, *The Chalice:*

In the year 1922, I was living in New York City and expecting my second child. With a combination of loneliness and sensitiveness, I began my real "tuning in" on the abstract experiences of the Inner Life.

Each day around two o'clock I went for a walk with my five-year-old daughter. As we came out of our brownstone house, I often noticed a little boy of about six who played on the sidewalk with other children. He had dark, olive skin, large burning eyes, a dirty face, and was ardent in every gesture. Each time he saw us, he would shyly try to approach me and my little girl.

One day after my period of study, my daughter and I left the house to take our usual walk to the Museum of Natural History, where we spent a good part of our time. As I walked down the steps, the boy came toward me—and I suddenly felt a rush of light penetrate my body. Raising his eyes and putting his arms about me, he said, "YOU ARE SO BEAUTIFUL."

How strange is repetition; how deep its lesson! Twenty years later my mother lay dying with cancer of the breast—a mother who had always resented being a mother. Now she lay in agony, experiencing her last retrospection. She had turned to Christian Science, and refused medical aid of any kind. On this day, as her passing came closer, I visited her in what had become a room of odors and impossible slow anguish. I had brought white roses from my garden, and when I placed them before her gaze, her face became illumined with maternal love. En rapport at last, the love between us became a white flame. As a brilliant light came into her Welsh face, her olive skin became luminous, her green eyes alight, and she said, "YOU ARE SO BEAUTIFUL."

These were the last words Ann Ree's mother spoke to her, for on the morning of the following day, Easter sunrise, death came. The day before her death, Ann Ree's mother became seriously concerned with the meaning of the Biblical statement, "Let us make man in our image" (Genesis 1:26). The plural "us" and "our" in this scriptural passage was not answered in her own religion and had remained a mystery to her. In the hours before the death coma, her consciousness was lucid and clear, and she began to discuss this Biblical passage with her daughter. Ann Ree explained that in the beginning of the earth's creation the Father was assisted by Great Beings called Elohim or Hierarchy. Her explanation of the dual, creative powers used by Hierarchy satisfied her mother and aided in relieving the last moments of tension.

Later that day Ann Ree made a special dedication, and prayed that she be given the ability to further clarify for herself and to others the system of duality working in the earth, and the part that pain plays in the soul-life of man. She also made a vow to devote herself to the teaching of the mercy aspect accompanying pain, and she prayed that she be shown the complete answer as to why so many in faith healing are not healed—and why many *are* healed; why some prayers are answered, while other prayers remain unanswered.

Soon after her mother's death Ann Ree had the experience of seeing the etheric presence of her mother on the steps of the funeral home where the physical body was being prepared for burial. Her mother was joyous and light. Showing Ann Ree how free she felt, she danced all around the entrance and foyer of the funeral home. Referring to the transition into death, her mother said, "There is simply nothing to it. There is simply nothing to it."

Her mother, having worked out the heavier pangs of purgatory through the fiery pain of cancer, was free—and a guest at her own funeral.

It was not yet Ann Ree's time to teach openly of the Masters. Thus she never mentioned the Masters from her pulpit, or that she was inspired through their instruction. Only to her closest pupils did she speak of these great Intermediary Beings who work with the Lord Jesus. Through her Inner-World experiences, she knew that when Jesus was on earth He was more than a Master and teacher; He was the World Saviour and Messiah, the only and true Door. She also knew that the Masters and other Presences of Heaven work with the Lord Jesus as ambassadors, and that they make possible telepathic communion between the invisible and visible worlds.

During the latter part of her ministry in Florida, when speaking to her larger audiences, there was always a feeling of compromise, in that she could not speak openly and freely of the realities within spiritual experience. The stony attitudes of those making investigative appraisals, and the non-understanding persons with rigid religious tenets, proved to be her cross. She would often spend a complete night weeping, because the unresponsiveness from such listeners was intuited and felt in her body.

There was a note of contest from certain religious groups and various ones in the city as Ann Ree's work continued to make progress as to healing and prophecy. Since early Christianity, religion has neglected the arts in the healing ministry, and, contradicting its prophetic origin, has been an arch foe of prophecy. The secular formalism within churches has suppressed and repressed all levels of prophecy, including the pure or spiritual prophecy.

There were those who feared Ann Ree and did all they could to destroy her reputation. Nevertheless, her work continued to increase, and her church continued to prosper.

Because her sermons drew large attendances, she was considered a dangerous rival by certain ministers who sought to silence her prophetic tongue. One prominent minister, who used his pulpit to speak against her, sometimes stationed himself outside her church and watched to see how many of his congregation attended her service.

When persons told me that my work was not sanctioned by their religion, I knew they were seeing my powers of revelation through bigotry. I knew that my spiritual powers were under the blessing of Heaven. These words of Paul were a continued comfort to me: "Despise not prophesyings. Prove all things; hold fast that which is good" (I Thessalonians 5:20, 21).

In addition to her being subjected to the prejudiced judgments of ecclesiastical bodies, there were always in the background the scepticisms of cynical-minded persons, the jealous undercurrents from spiritistic societies, and the subtle, hypnotic persecutions by certain occult leaders and groups.

Persons who were interested only in her prophetic visions were chagrined and frustrated when she suggested to them that they depend upon their souls and apply themselves to the philosophical and spiritual truths. More than one person said to her, "I have all the virtues. Why can't I do what you do?" Some would ask her, "Why don't you use your powers to get rich?" Ann Ree never prayed for personal gain or possessions, for she knew that such prayers were selfish and offended a spiritual ethic.

There were those who did not know how to classify her work, and often referred to her powers as being psychical. However, she knew that her work was beyond the psychical.

Untrained persons who know not the difference between the psychical and the spiritual would try to identify my gifts as being "ESP." This definition discomforted me, for I knew there was a wide difference between spasmodic, fragmentary, psychical experiences and the intelligible continuity of spiritual experiences.

There are psychic energies which are as dangerous as raw electricity. I had seen many persons unwittingly expose themselves to the danger of psychic energies. I had seen their lives wrecked and their mentalities distorted.

I was disturbed when people wanted to classify my

work as psychical. Since my early years I had refused to be trapped into psychic enticements, for I had received a greater and benign blessing resulting from spiritual powers.

The popular research into ESP is a desire to prove that there are existing phenomena beyond man's exterior consciousness. However, science has yet to divulge the soul resources of the Spirit.

Persons who are interested in psychic phenomena seek excitation and sensation. A too intense research into psychic phenomena opens the psychic portals in the subconscious level of the brain and exposes one to the human and astral undercurrents of inverted telepathy.

If a person has spiritual grace from a former life, he knows inwardly the difference between the psychical and the spiritual. In the beginning of his soul-searching he may be exposed to the psychical pitfalls; however, through grace he has the power of discrimination which protects him and shields him.

If a person has grace, and is inadvertently drawn into the orbit of psychic exploration, he cannot endure for longer than a three-year period the subtleties accompanying psychic experience. His grace enables him to move beyond the psychical into the spiritual.

I have seen repeatedly the superiority of the spiritual over the psychical. The spiritual endows one with a benign blessing, while the psychical diverts a person from the rhythm of his soul. The psychical keeps alive the primitive elements of one's nature; the spiritual illumines the mind, opens the heart, and produces order and creation.

The continued cross-current from doubting and interrogating persons, combined with her heavy labors of teaching and the ministry, exhausted Ann Ree physically and kept her constantly on the defensive so as to protect her gifts. Finally, she came to the decision that she would no longer serve the public in the same way, but would seek her own peace and evolvement. It was then that Master M came to her and gave the first key to her freedom from the burden of secrecy and repression carried since childhood.

In January 1945, a few days after she underwent a serious operation, Ann Ree was told by the Master that she was ready to close her large church. He stated that in the approaching eleven years she would prepare herself to prophesy on a universal level and no longer concern herself with the "human karmas" of others. He said that her spiritual powers, for the balance of her life, would be used for prophecies pertaining to cosmos realities or the universal concerns of men, and that she would teach openly of the little-known sources of Spiritual Mediation, among these, the angels and the Masters.

Ann Ree did not immediately obey the Master's guidance to close her church, but continued her ministry due to the needs and demands of the loved ones in her work. After returning to her church work and its burdens, she fainted in the pulpit on three consecutive Sundays; on the day following the third Sunday, she lost the use of her voice.

A Being of Mediation never makes a decision for the disciple. Decisions are left entirely to the disciple's own will. Even though the Master had said that her work in the church had reached its fulfillment, by the right of choice she still had the opportunity to make the final decision. Through the loss of her voice, and the physical inability to carry on her work, Ann Ree received a direct answer as to what was expected of her, and she realized that she had touched a greater Will than her own will and the wills of those associated with her.

The following month, June 1945, her voice returned, and under guidance from the Master she went to the Pocono mountains in Pennsylvania. Free from the demands of others, she rebuilt her physical and etheric bodies with careful diet and by walking eight or more miles each day, regardless of the weather. Through her study of the Bible, and the rhythmic practice of meditation, she began another phase of alignment with the Worlds of Mediation.

In the Western world, spiritual dedication is a rarity. It is the nature of the Western disciple to be caught up into many extrovert affairs and many crowded events. These diverting impulses and interesting by-paths come between him and dedication. Sickness comes to the Western disciple as a restraining element, so that he might come closer to his soul, and reach a sustained momentum in the Light. Thus, to the Western disciple, sickness is a door to initiation and illumination.

Every spiritual illumination I have ever experienced has come after a serious sickness.

In the last month of my fourteenth year, I became critically ill with typhoid fever. Several months later, at the end of my convalescence, I knew on Easter Sunday that I must sever my ties with traditional religion, and thereafter follow the light of my soul. I was never again to be affiliated with any personal source of religious or spiritual instruction. My training was received solely through my inner hearing and visions.

In New York City, during the birth of my second child, I came perilously close to losing my life. After her birth, I began to follow the light of the Masters and to live within the glow of their instruction. During the next twenty years I maintained a balance in the health of my physical body.

In my forty-fifth year I underwent gall bladder surgery and was not expected to live. While in the hospital I experienced the Polar-Lights Initiation, and heard the Music of the Spheres playing upon the magnetic poles of the earth. My lesser etheric body was healed through these tones. During my recuperation the Master instructed me to relinquish the heavier demands of my ministry, and prepare to teach a handful of God. *Until my forty-fifth year my deeper visions of Heaven had been kept secret, but after this time I spoke openly of my visions and of Heaven.*

I have always had a tremendous love of life and a vigorous inner strength to overcome sicknesses and weaknesses. One's love of life, I am told, can be used by the angels in their ministering helps. I have been too outgoing to live a life of austerity. I have invited penalties upon my health because I have not known when to stop giving of myself. To see a need, and to know that I held some of the answers to the need, exacted a great toll from my strength. There was neither enough time nor energy to do all my heart told me I must do.

When Ann Ree returned to Florida in December 1945, she established a library and reading room. The next year she built a beautiful chapel on the lot adjoining her home, and began to teach the deeper or esoteric truths, the Bible being the chief source for instruction.

Since her thirty-third year Ann Ree had been trained in the recovering of the soul-records of past lives. In 1945 she united herself with the record of her just previous life. Her conflict in accepting the record of this former life—its memory and its burdens—enabled her to understand why certain persons will not accept the fact that they have had other lives; they sense that their acceptance of past-life records will accelerate their meeting the negative actions of their former lives.

During this period several of her students also experienced visions and dreams which revealed their teacher's previous life.

In the reading of her soul's embodiment records, Ann Ree was shown that her work—through the years of counseling, healing, and teaching—was a means of expiating her own karma of five former lives before she could extract the grace from these lives as power, and re-align her personality to the Christ. She was also shown that by having served thousands of persons she had prepared herself to open the akasic records of humanities, nations, and continents, and to tap the memory-record of the creation of the earth.

4

The Initiatory Years

And I have heard of thee, that thou canst make interpretations, and dissolve doubts.

—Daniel 5:16

In the year of 1944 Ann Ree received her first communication from Thomas Sugrue, author of many published works, including the book *There is a River*—the biography of Edgar Cayce. Mr. Sugrue wrote that he had heard of her powers and was anxious to meet her. A short time later he invited her to visit him during his stay in Clearwater Beach, Florida; however, her work and health at this time prevented an immediate contact. In April 1945, Thomas Sugrue came to her home in St. Petersburg. This was the beginning of a friendship lasting until the day of his death.

Thomas Sugrue became interested in every phase of Ann Ree's work. He was especially interested in the prophetic and healing aspects of her teaching, and in her interpretation of the Bible. He said that her church was similar to the churches of early Christianity, and described her teachings as "pure gnosis."

During the next four years, whenever Thomas Sugrue came to Florida, Ann Ree visited him twice a week at his home in Clearwater Beach. Here they discussed endless subjects, personal and universal. Thomas Sugrue was always the newspaper man, and, concerning her work, he was an observer. His interest in Ann Ree centered around the fact that she had powers of precognition and clairvoyance without using any form of trance or hypnosis—and that she spontaneously and fluently produced the answers to his every approach in questioning. They spent many hours at dusk—his favorite time—discussing the future of man, the dangers of the age, and the world events affecting mankind.

Thomas Sugrue urged Ann Ree to write of her experiences. He began gathering data on her life, for it was his plan to eventually write of her work. The last time they met, he stated emphatically: "Put down everything that happens to you. What is happening to you does not belong to you; it belongs to the world. Get a number 2 pencil, a yellow legal-size pad, and write something every day. THEY will help you!"

One midnight in October 1948, Master M awakened Ann Ree and instructed her to go to Oceanside, California. Here she would meet Mrs. Max Heindel of the Rosicrucian Fellowship before the elderly Mrs. Heindel passed out of the body.

Having no connections or affiliations with the Rosicrucian Fellowship, Ann Ree arrived in Oceanside as a visitor. Within a short period of time she became a channel for the healing of a woman suffering from a bowel condition caused by the sphincter muscle's having been severed during surgery. This brought Ann Ree's healing powers to the attention of certain members of the Board of Directors, and she was asked to visit Mrs.

Max Heindel, who had not been well since a previous operation. During these daily visits, which continued into December 1948, Mrs. Heindel became very fond of Ann Ree and affectionately referred to her as "the woman with the beautiful eyes."

In my visits with Mrs. Heindel I noticed a large woven sampler of the Twenty-third Psalm above the headboard of her bed. Since childhood I had used the Twenty-third Psalm to expand my communion with the angels. I told Mrs. Heindel that I had discovered that each sign of the zodiac correlated to one of the verses of this great Psalm. She was delighted when I revealed to her that the first house sign of the zodiac correlated to the words, "The Lord is my shepherd," and that the second line, "I shall not want," correlated to Taurus, etc. I told her that I used the Twenty-third Psalm each day at dusk to retrospect and observe the used-up hours of the day. I described how I began my retrospection by speaking the words of the Psalm while visualizing the zodiacal signs. This practice helped me to review my day's actions and thoughts.

Mrs. Heindel, who gave the hardihood of her physical labors to many persons lost in the miasma-mist of occultism, was a strong soul, indomitable. In her late years she was not understood by many who had been absent in the shoulder-to-shoulder trials of the Fellowship. I will always remember her with an ephemeris in her hand looking out upon the grounds of the former bean patch where now stood the temples of devotion.

While at the Fellowship, Ann Ree met her own "threshold dweller," and knew him to be the obstacle to her further progress. During a three-day period of an unnamed illness of fevers and pain, she mastered and dissolved this dweller.

The archaic dweller of my former wrong actions appeared to me as a decaying visage. He gave off a repugnant odor of decay and death. I knew him to be an entity formed by my own errors and misdemeanors. In this three-day experience I relived shocking things of other ages and times. On the fourth day I felt like a soul ascended up from hell.

One day while standing outside the temple of Mount Ecclesia, Ann Ree was contemplating the unknown years ahead; suddenly, a voice of thunder proceeded out of the all-seeing eye directly over the entrance to the temple. At the same moment an electric-like current penetrated the center of her forehead. In this second she knew that she had received an anointing by the Holy Ghost. From that moment forward, her apostle powers began.

I had sought companionship with my contemporaries at the Rosicrucian Fellowship, but after this Holy Ghost experience, I knew that the Rosicrucian Fellowship was not my spiritual home, and that the world was now awaiting a spiritual rather than a philosophical teaching.

Before returning to Florida, Ann Ree received the first clear indication of her future work. Master M appeared and said to her, "You will form a spiritual Guild, and teach pure ethics."

In 1949 Ann Ree was introduced to Dr. E., a teacher of the Rudolf Steiner organization, Anthroposophy. Dr. E., then in her eighties, had been a personal friend of Edouard Schuré and Rudolf Steiner. She was a distinguished Doctor of Science and a prominent artist.

The meeting between Dr. E. and myself was arranged by a student of mine who brought people together so that she might observe their reaction to one another. However, Dr. E. and I grew very fond of each other, and during the next three years we were to have many long discussions.

Dr. E. helped me to clarify my own motives and to come closer to my true dedication. I loved this courageous and inspired woman who epitomized the woman-initiate of an ending era. I realized that the scientific age would produce a different type of woman-initiate, and that occult laws which had previously sustained initiation were to be replaced by spiritual ethic.

I saw that the initiates of the coming era would change the course of religion.

Having a small group of select students whom she taught through the Platonic technique of discussion, Dr. E. produced tangible results in both the spiritual and the outer expression of her students. She did not involve herself in the karma of her students, but freed them to their own judgments and the action within their own karmas. Her classical spirituality was a rarity in a materialistic age.

In 1949 Ann Ree had profound spiritual experiences with three mighty Beings of the Higher Worlds.

During the summer solstice of 1949, I went to the Gulf and immersed myself in the water. While in the water, I began to pray, and as I prayed I felt the deep need to offer myself up for world-service. When I turned to go back to shore, the clouds in the sky appeared to foam and boil, and a tremendous sound issued forth. It was similar to the sound of an iceberg cracking on the surface. A figure formed in the foamy mist of the sky, and instantly I knew in my mind that the figure seen was called Lanoo. As he manifested his full form, he spoke to me and said in thunderous, awesome, loving tones, "You are loved."

On this solstice day my mind became united with his mind, and I was taught of the waters of the world: the oceans, the rivers, the streams. The inner significance of the blood stream of man was opened to me, and I understood the spiritual power within the blood; I learned why some men have natural alliances with one another, and why others have antipathies toward one another. It was on this day that I was initiated into the life-stream of the humanities, and learned of the great life-tides within the human spirit.

During the winter solstice of 1949, while I was meditating in my study that day, I had my first vision of the Ancient of Days. He appeared seated on a fiery cloud surrounded by white-blue flames. The vision of this Divine Being prepared me for my initiation into timing and into rhythm. From the Ancient of Days I learned of the soul's timing, of destiny timing, and of karmic timing. I also learned of acceptable times, when men receive great spiritual blessings from Heaven and are caught up into destinies more noble than can be contemplated by the human mind.

During the ending of my ministry in Florida, I experienced heavy human sorrow. The dying to an established life came hard to my nature. On every side, I was met by challenges, defeats and dead-ends—for I was being shepherded toward a new way which would *provide me with immeasurable joy. One day when I was depressed and despondent due to my dying to the old way, the Mother of Jesus appeared to me in a vision. She was surrounded by a blue medallion, and gave off an inner light similar to the angels. In her left arm she held her Babe, and raised her right hand in a blessing, saying to me, "Fret not thyself because of evildoers."*

After this blessing from Mary, I experienced a renewal, a rejuvenation, and accepted the new way before me. From her spiritual presence came a holy emanation, and I knew inwardly that if her Son could bear His suffering, I too would be given the strength to rise over my suffering.

After relinquishing her ministry in Florida, Ann Ree returned to California, where she experienced a humility initiation and a thorough self-research. In these days of self-searching she came face to face with her Guardian Angel and was shown her flaws and frailties. She often doubted whether she would ever teach again, and she questioned her own worth as a prophet.

Friends in California advised her to return to her spiritual work. One dear friend, who had frequent flashes of inspired insight, said to her, "Only by returning to your spiritual teaching will you regain peace."

The humility initiation continued until Ann Ree received a renewed prophetic anointing. Gradually, the wider portals of illumination opened to her heart, mind, and soul. She moved beyond a personal chaos into a craftsman-like research of the Higher Worlds. Her revelation powers became coordinated, and she diligently fulfilled her rhythms of meditation. Even though she felt the tremors of human affairs, she continued to live a life of positive union with Heaven.

As part of her resolving of the past, and preparation for the future, Ann Ree burned thousands of written testimonials that she had received over a period of sixteen years. She knew that the testimonials remained in the sacred confines of the memories of those who had experienced miraculous healings and had witnessed things beyond their mortal sense. She also knew that such records are written eternally and never die.

In the reading of my soul-records I learned that I had been of the Catholic faith in the last three lives. During the period of my dying to the old, I sometimes found myself with a hunger to be embodied in a religion offering security and peace.

In Santa Barbara, California, I often visited the Mission during the late afternoon mass. I found a sanctity in the prayers of those who had surrendered themselves to their beliefs; however, I knew that I could never affiliate myself with crystallized formulas. During this time there were occasions when I heard inwardly a chorus of voices saying, "Come back to the church. Come back to the church."

My conflict between past-life worship habits and present-life convictions lasted for three months. This conflict was the forerunner of an illness I was to experience at Easter. Immediately after this illness I came under the instruction of the Ancient Phoenician or Master R. I learned under his tutelage that all religions are to undergo a cleansing and purging. This has proven to be so, for in every walk of religion may now be seen a self-searching and a requalification to religious covenants.

One day when I was meditating in a very beautiful garden in Santa Barbara, I saw a vision of an eagle flying. The eagle—the symbol of initiation—was blue in color. From the eagle's breast fell one drop of blood to the earth. While I was seeing the vision, I was told that every person who has a spiritual life must give of his heart, must open his heart, and his heart must bleed. This vision came to me during a time when I was undergoing intense suffering, and it was a most comforting symbol to see.

I contributed to much of my own suffering and sorrow. Having a strong will, I had yet to fully understand that my life was not under my own direction. Whatever I would choose or desire through human affection was removed from my life. My destiny would shake loose anything I tried to hold or claim.

Until I became whole as a prophet, I knew very little human happiness. Only when I reached the fruition of my spiritual powers did happiness visit me. However, my truest joy was in my spiritual work—and, at last, when I saw the fruits of my work, this was joy.

All prophets must in some degree undergo the Job initiatory trials. Even as Job in the Bible, they are exposed to the danger of losing their family, their monies, their health, and their honor. I experienced each of these in my formative prophetic years. I lost my family in my late twenties, my monies in my early thirties; my health was impaired and my honor was endangered in my forties. As the years went by, I regained family, money, and recognition. However, my health has been in a precarious balance since my forties. The inner sensitivities and the struggles which make up a prophet's life have exacted a heavy toll from my physical health.

Dr. Gene Cosgrove, an advanced spiritual teacher, was the last person to aid Ann Ree in the transition from her past labors to the new work awaiting her. When they met each other for the first time, they had the simultaneous experience of seeing Master M in majestic height over one another. So powerful was the impact of the experience that they both burst into tears.

Her meeting with Dr. Cosgrove in Santa Barbara, California was an intantaneous recognition of catalyst disciples. From their association Ann Ree recalled former lives in France, in which they had influenced the destiny of the French people.

Dr. Cosgrove, author of *The Disciple,* was an unselfish and devoted teacher who had dedicated his life to small groups throughout the world. At one time, he had been a close associate of Alice Bailey, but had withdrawn from her teachings so that he might bring to his students a better understanding of the Christ.

Dr. Cosgrove helped Ann Ree to understand the "why" of her just previous years when he said to her, "You are undergoing synthesis—and changing to the other Rays of Hierarchy." She was later to learn, through her own research, that synthesis for the new-age disciple concerned not only the Rays of Hierarchy, but the "Light-Streams" of the Masters.

Until her meeting with Dr. Cosgrove in December 1950, Ann Ree had been in telepathic alignment with Master M. However, before a disciple may do a universal work, he must command or incorporate all of the seven telepathic Light-Streams of the Masters; for there are, at this time, seven great intermediary channelings through which the Masters send their telepathic ideas to the world. To gain synthesis within the Light-Streams, the disciple must unite with the soul records of the present life and several former lives. This was experienced by Ann Ree between 1943 and 1950.

When the seven differentiated Light-Streams become part of the disciple's telepathic mediation, he is then initiated into the twelve ethics as established by the Lord Jesus. These ethics are the source of all true teaching and healing.

While living in Santa Barbara in March 1951, Ann Ree became seriously ill with pneumonia and knew that death could come at any moment. During the crucial hours of her sickness she had an exhausting and terrifying experience with the subtle or satanic worlds. For two hours she struggled with subtle assailants who sought to draw her higher etheric body downward through her feet into the anterior worlds. She knew that the true way to leave the physical body is through the crown of the head. If her assailants had won, she would have died as a victim of the dark. When the battle was finally over, she kept full command of her higher etheric body. This victory enabled her to overcome the fear of death and to enter into a peaceful acceptance of God's Will.

Immediately after her victory over the satanic assailants, Ann Ree heard the voice of Master M saying, "You can go—and you are ready, if you want to go . . . " She knew that he was referring to her death. Then she was shown a vision of her next life on earth.

His voice continued, " . . . or you can choose to remain." Ann Ree replied, "I am not ready to go. I have something yet to finish. I must go back to Florida; something is waiting for me there." She did not know what it was she had to finish, or why she felt she must return to Florida.

Within a short period of time Ann Ree realized that she had passed an important test, for after she made the choice to remain in the world she became increasingly aware of the telepathic Light-Stream of the "Great Phoenician," or Master R. Master R, channeling his telepathy through the seventh Light-Stream, holds the key to the survival of religions in the world. He also enables the dedicated disciple to make synthesis, or to blend with all seven telepathic Light-Streams of the Masters.

One of the first symbolic lessons I received from the Great Phoenician, or Master R, was the parable of the awkward disciple. In a vision I saw the loving, benign and kindly Master R seated upon a triad-like dais. He was weaving a basket. As he worked on the basket, tying and shaping the threads, he instructed the handful of disciples seated in an orderly fashion below the dais. Each disciple at his feet also held a basket and was engrossed in weaving his basket under the Master's direction. Suddenly, as if by a strong wind, the door flew open and an untidy, unkempt person entered the room. He moved from disciple to disciple inspecting and scrutinizing each basket. Through the room there moved a concerted repulsion for this untidy one. The eyes of the Master were filled with love and compassion. The unkempt disciple became aware of his own awkwardness, and he became calm in the proximity of the Master's love. He quietly took his place among the other disciples and began to weave his basket. The Master said in soft tones, "This is the lesson of the awkward disciple. His mind is unkempt; he is concerned only with the work of other disciples, rather than his own. Before a disciple enters the door to the Master, he must learn repose, and he must also learn diligence, that he may quietly and unassumingly take up his task of weaving his spiritual garment."

The Great Phoenician is the master of parables, rituals, and symbols. It was necessary for me in the training in synthesis to extend my knowledge of formulas and symbols, for my future work required that I be well-versed in the root ideas and symbols sustaining all religious bodies.

The pneumonia suffered by Ann Ree in California followed a powerful illumination she had experienced after teaching a series of Easter lessons. This sickness proved to be one of the last cleansings designed to release her from emotional congestion.

The illuminative state of consciousness returned during her convalescence. Her past studies and research gave her the ability to estimate the worth of the ideas that were coming to her, and she realized that she had tapped a new vein of spiritual knowledge. She knew these ideas to be spiritual gold and valuable assets to the spiritual life. However, she became disturbed and concerned when the downpouring of illuminative ideas began to come so rapidly that she could not write them or retain them. It was in this period that she saw a vision of a young man, and asked, "What have I to do with that young man? I do not know him." She was told by Master M that there was someone in Florida who would help her.

Until this time Ann Ree had written pure "freshet sentences," but she had yet to earn the spiritual competence to write and speak sacred mantrams. One day during her dusk contemplation in Santa Barbara, she released herself from her physical body and traveled etherically to the surrounding hills of the city. Looking downward upon the lighted windows of the houses, she received her first mantram correlating to the sacred word-formulas of Heaven.

Mighty is the Love,
The arc of power in life;
Love, the breath of the exalted space.
Mighty is the Light;
The merging, penetrable,
The moving, the extendable,
Increasing Light.
Mighty is the Word;
The sound going forth,
The call going out.
Mighty, mighty, mighty, the Word.
Mighty is the Power,
Increasing in Love,
In Light,
In speech.
The need,

The call,
The activity.
The Love,
The Light,
The Word,
The Power.

One day, while meditating with a dear friend in a small park, Ann Ree was aware of a swift-moving body of water beneath her feet. She told her friend that in the very near future a river would be discovered running beneath the park. Three years later this was confirmed, for engineers building a dam twenty miles north discovered a subterranean river and traced its current through the area where Ann Ree and her friend had meditated.

The friends I met during my spiritual rehabilitation constantly concerned themselves for my good. These friends had succored me through physical illness and through harsh blows. They were dear to me in a deep spiritual sense. One day two of my friends decided that we should take a trip to the Ojai valley. On this day we packed our lunch and drove to Ojai; we went to a park-like place on the Wheeler Springs Road and sat by a small clear brook. Before lunch we began to talk about Nature and the spiritual life. While we were talking, I observed a dying tree a few feet away, and then the tree came alive with small, golden, etheric birds similar to hummingbirds. These birds danced from limb to limb singing certain special notes, and I saw the root-fire in the tree being drawn up into the branches. I was told inwardly that these birds were the golden mending birds *who work to keep alive the life-germ of vegetation.*

At the moment of Wesak in May 1951, Ann Ree experienced an initiation of fire and light during meditation. In this initiation, each point of light in her body projected from itself a vast, whirling flame which resolved itself into light. This was the last stage in consuming any egotism that remained in her, and was the final initiation of its kind required before she could receive greater disclosures of the Heaven Worlds.

5
Stefan

But when ye shall hear of wars and commotions, be not terrified: for these things must first come to pass; but the end is not by and by.

—St. Luke 21:9

In the spring of 1951 Ann Ree became concerned about the Korean war and its needless slaughter. One day, while in full consciousness, she released herself from her physical body, and found herself with Master R on a battlefield in Korea. She saw a wounded American soldier, and was told that his name was Stefan.

The officer in command and the buddies of Stefan believed him to be frozen and dead. On losing consciousness, Stefan found himself in the etheric realms with the Ancient Phoenician or Master R. For three days and nights he relived his life through the eyes of the "Phoenician." Before returning to physical consciousness, Stefan was instructed to seal into his mind what he had experienced, so that he could "aid the many leaning in this direction."

The thoughts and pictures that moved through the mind of Stefan were transcribed by Ann Ree. The following passages are from her diary of Stefan's thoughts:

The light was different; and first I thought, "It's too quiet," and I felt as if I were above the ground. I couldn't see any of the others around. I seemed to be on top of a place among small hilltops, thinking of how the snow was blue-white, not like the dirt and smell and the noises that come to hurt your ears. I seemed to be alone, no guns or yelling—just a clean, restful quiet.

Then I suddenly knew I wasn't alone, for standing to my right was a man. I knew he wasn't Chinese, Korean, or Russian. I don't know how I knew—and he wasn't U.S.A. either.

First I thought, "This is a priest—I am dead." Then, as I tried to straighten it out, he came over and just looked at me. I had a sort of crazy feeling. As he looked at me my body began to get warm and light; my thoughts began to tell me things about the place—for I knew then I was on top of a mountain and the other fellows weren't anywhere near, and I thought, "I *am* dead!" He smiled and spoke, and even though he says I'll forget almost all that happened, I'll never forget the *sound* of his voice. It was gentle and strong, soft and clear—it was a voice that made me think, "Well, if I'm dead, it's all right; and wonder what had there been after all to be afraid about." "Yes," said the Phoenician, "it's like that." (That's what he later told me to call him.) I had a feeling of trust and quiet inside. I *knew* him; I had always known him.

Then, suddenly, I was walking alongside him. My parka was off my head. I could feel the air; it was clean and exciting. Every part of me seemed free and light.

For weeks I had been so damn tired. We had crawled; and walked; and sometimes tried to get a lift on one of the trucks—but the legs are what get you: the legs and the eyes. You look until you can't look any more. You walk and walk and don't know where you are walking. It was so good to feel free—out of that. I thought suddenly, "I didn't fit here."

The Phoenician smiled. I knew later he knew everything I was thinking. We moved along fast and free, almost like flying. Suddenly before us I saw a craggy-like rock. We turned in. I thought first the walls were snow; then I saw it was rock, and made a sort of corridor into an aisle or crossing. He called this "the *crevice.*"

The walls about us were dry and gave off a feeling as if you are going into a house where people are waiting. It seemed as if there were other people near by; and the Phoenician hurried ahead of me a little. We then crossed another crevice; we walked over that through a large door into a hall-like place. The Phoenician said, "Wait, Steve." I seemed to think it was all right for him to know my name. How he knew didn't seem to bother me—even the boys call me "Gorsky," not Steve. And my folks call me Stefan. The only ones who ever called me

Steve were Chrissy, and my aunt-in-law (when I was a little boy).

Chrissy is the daughter of the Lithuanian printer I tried to work for back home. I first knew my aunt-in-law when I was about five; she was important in our family for a long time. She helped us all. Anastasia, my mother, said she was a philosopher, or a wise woman. My aunt changed our family's thoughts on religion a lot. She called me Steve because she said it was American, and I must be every bit American.

My mother, Anastasia, was White Russian, and Roman Catholic. She came to this country as a young girl because her mother did not want her to be Greek Orthodox. She is quiet and peaceful; and she is confused in religion. She made us all go to mass, but she never talked about it much.

I never thought much about religion. We all knew it was better to be good; and we all knew that what Anastasia didn't lick out of us we got from Father—in confession.

I signed up in the Marines with my buddy Ed; he got it just three weeks after we got out there. And I had been mixed up inside ever since. There was something about the Phoenician that made me know I was going to get a lot of the answers, and feel better about them. I had the feeling of having almost everything I had asked for, but was still alert to something wonderful and good about to happen.

Suddenly, something clicked in my mind; I knew where we were. From that moment I stopped asking questions—and as he told me later, time was short for me to get all I had to get. We were in the high Himalayas, the Sacred Mountains the boys had been talking about—just sort of the way you talk about ghosts, confessions, and girls. You don't believe all those things even though you want to believe them. There had been so much talk among some of the fellows about religion. We had one guy who was studying for his degree when he signed up. He said in this range of mountains there had always been a mystery; always drew people—and sometimes people went into them and never came out; and some tried to go in, and something no one could explain kept them out—they would be sent back in disgrace for not "making the grade."

When we were in Tokyo waiting for big Mac to put us in, Sergeant MacGregor (little Mac to us) told a story after the big earthquake—that it was the sign of God's displeasure with the sins of man. Now I know, from what the Phoenician said, that it is not just the sins of the Tibetans and people nearby, but of the whole earth. And now, while I was waiting, I knew this was a sacred place—like a church; but more than that, you didn't feel guilty and uneasy as in a church: you felt as if you had always known there was such a place, and would find it.

"You are not dead," said the Phoenician. "You are in your etheric body. It is a body larger than your physical body, but exactly like your physical body; it is part of your physical body, but of a finer substance. When you go back to life in your world, you will have a friend sent to you to teach you about the bodies. What you learn here is to prepare you for a work—for you are through with the war. The injury you have received will make it impossible for you to fight again. Someday you will know it was the best thing to happen to you; for it is through this that you will find your real self and your real work. After this, you will not find it so hard to place yourself; or to accept what you find around you in the world.

"Because of your wound . . . " Then a picture appeared before me as on a motion picture screen. I saw my body against the little hill where I'd been when the ground went out. I looked into the chest, into the lung—a bloody hole—and three ribs cracked. It wasn't too good. My body looked dead: the head twisted to the side; my arms spread out; my knees were drawn up.

The Phoenician said, "You will be found by the medics. Your wound will heal, but you will always be weak in this part of your body. And you will have, as a compensation, an understanding opened up to you; for any injury to, or trouble with, the lungs destroys race prejudice, and brings understanding of mankind.

"For three days you will remain here with me; in this time, you will recover such records of other lives as are needed by you for your coming work; and you will be briefed as to the rational pattern within the cause of things. The rest is up to you—for discovery is part of your soul's work.

"No one comes to this part of the etheric regions unless he has earned it in other times, other lives. It is part of the present war's phenomena that the wounded—when qualified by past-life spiritual acts—are given certain inner instructions toward the helping in the new times ahead for men.

"The increasing pressure of man's devouring man builds a wall. And there are too few who can penetrate the spiritual strata. Because you developed a strong prayer-body in your last life, it is possible for you to experience the things waiting to be taught from this area."

As we were speaking I felt the approach of another being who seemed familiar; and as the Phoenician spoke I suddenly felt my mind advance to a peculiar state. I was with a friend—one who had been with me in a village in Poland, yes Poland, in this "other time" of which the Phoenician spoke. I could see a small stream of water nearby, a study or a walled room with books, and two men talking. I was aware that this friend was trying to remonstrate with me to not be rash in my views. As the vision unfolded,

I saw myself as having been persecuted by the Russians for my strength in Poland. I saw that the time element was in the seventeenth century. Before this austere and kindly friend faded from sight, he told me that I had been looking for recognition. When the vision ended, I felt in my mind a sort of ache and hunger to speak further; to feel once again that closeness. Also still lingering in my mind was the feeling of hopeless reasoning against some blind inhuman force, of which I had been victim.

"Yes," said the Phoenician, "you are in this war because you have a tie with the war-forces set loose on earth; but the remorse and regret you feel show that you have modified these errors through the manner of your death in the last life. The Polish life which brought so much pain was built by yourself, for in a previous Russian life you abused authority and persecuted the weak."

Suddenly I saw a group of Cossack soldiers riding upon a ghetto or enclosure of the Jewish; it was, I felt, a scene in Vilna. Destruction, whips, fire, mockery—all rode across my mind's vision and body with a feeling of shame, for I recognized one of the Cossacks as myself.

The Phoenician said, "As long as shame is felt for a deed long done, the karmic tie still exists in the time of now. So may you read and remember, my son.

"You are now American, Steve; and you are

at war. So we stop here, to see at last, the circle within the circle that is man and his life on earth.

"You are one among the millions of souls who have reached a karmic ripeness in preparation for a new age.

"In human governments, until now, there has been a necessity to widen the orbit of man's energies. Unfortunately, this has distracted him from his noble qualities.

"Though man often thinks he is separate from God, God and man are never separate. There is now a crisis in which the Spiritual Ones behind the curtain of man's darkness work as they have never worked before.

"Bitter is the blood mixed with the gall of wasted time. Misused energy is misused wisdom. Creation without God is congestion to God's system. Man now has reached a place which says, 'Stop! . . . Cease!'

"In your country, Steve, there are great canyon gardens which were once part of a great cosmic action; they are the beautiful reminders of man's impotence against the power of destiny. Today there are spots of activity in which men, by skillful enterprise, have built great cities; they too, in time, shall perish.

"Men are not pawns, nor are they helpless. Each person on earth is possessed of *will* which he must learn to use purely.

"The laws of karma invoke their penalties upon those who use malicious wills. Karmic retribution is a final, irrevocable law. Sometimes this does not exact its full consequence in one life, but is balanced in a sequence of several lives.

"Evil becomes an entity created by man's continuous willful perversions. This entity, as a world menace, now overshadows all mankind. This entity has been built over many hundreds of years. Having devoted the powers of his mind to materialistic gain, man now finds his instinctive good being overwhelmed by inventive destruction.

"Man is not at war so much with a people, race or political body, as with something created by the consent of the many.

"The Presences of the Inner Worlds stand by to aid in the spiritual birth of man, to bring light to darkness, to bring cleansing from fire, to replace terror with trust, and to give healing for pain.

"This etheric mountain pass is a pivot polarity, an ether-ingress into humanity; it is in exact alignment with the place known to the world as Tibet. In this etheric polarity the spiritual Presences have worked to aid men in leadership in many walks of life.

"The precious metals of the world are always indicative of an orbit of spiritual power. In your America the great west has produced the gold of that continent. Wherever you see gold in large quantities, Spirit has a body through which to work.

"When men in polarity points prove unworthy to receive the spiritual outpouring from the Higher Worlds, the Greater Presences withdraw their proximity—and the former polarity points become battlegrounds where men shed their blood.

"When men resign themselves to the sound of men walking in the boots of war, deep under men's feet the earth is being shaken; the core of this planet is being strained to its fiery depths. Those who are pure in intent will survive to create a new world, upon which God has His hand.

"Courage is never lost; ideals, if they are earnestly believed on, survive as strength in the soul. There are brave men today, as there have been brave men in all ages; but it is not enough to be brave with a clouded view into the whole of things. Of the brave much more will be asked than the going into war.

"Streaming into the ether-crucible are many like you, Steve, who are the little avatars of a new people. The continents will change; viewpoints, culture, creation—all will have greater expression.

"This age will be known as *the Convulsions of the Continents.*

"This is a war without hate—a war of wrangling inconsistencies resulting from the churning emotions in the world."

As the Phoenician continued, the walls about us were alive with pictures of his words. Each idea became an object shaking me with the force of pictures characterized. I could see how such power made it possible for memory to remain imprinted in me; and how memories of a past life were ironed or molded into each of us—to be brought back to live as a sort of over-directing or super-consciousness. All of the wonder had changed to a charged, happy truth in every part of me.

The Phoenician smiled, not with his lips or eyes, but with a light blazing out of him. "What a Being," I thought. The Phoenician, answering my thoughts, said, "No, Steve, there are others far greater, carrying a greater light than I. Before the story of Solomon was written into the Book you call the Old Testament, I lived as an initiate in the days of Tyre. I was known as the Ancient Phoenician or Hiram Abiff. I now use the Hiram Abiff form because it harmonizes with the vibration of the masses of humanity who are turning in vast numbers in the direction upward. I have prepared many initiates. I work with you to etch into your memory the truth about the upper etheric spheres—which are to become accessible to man, if he passes his test in the crucial trial before him. Should the forces of darkness tilt the continents, another great day of darkness would come on all lands encircling the earth. Man would lose for many thousands of years the use of continuity in consciousness. The souls of men seek to free them from the mist of deluded omnipotence.

"Men have experimented with the powers of will for billions of years. They now will become aware of the power within the thought world. They will come to understand space and time.

"Previous to this century it was the custom to gather together at intervals a select few and initiate them into the mysteries of other spheres or planes. Their participation in the world-mysteries was carried over from body to body or life to life. In the present age there is a new impetus for initiation; many who have little knowledge of the mysteries will now place their feet upon the first rung of the ladder of initiation.

"Within the pivot of the earth every form of life is being drawn upward in a mighty surge of power. Union with God is the purpose of the plan.

"The Molten Sea, or the fiery core of the earth, contains the destroying archetypal tones. These tones now work to dissolve the old; but before these changes are fulfilled, man must cross the 'Red Sea'—the sea of tumults in the blood. When this occurs, the forces working through blood and race will be sealed away; and another form of action in the blood of man will come, producing a new type of mind. Thus, the Inner-World governings will be given more freedom for their work.

"All egos or souls embodied in the races are in a preparatory crucible for the new age—a new age which will produce men who will live on earth in a rarified atmosphere. With the aid of the Higher Beings, men will use their spiritual powers to spiritualize the very soil of the earth.

"Reverent men with spiritual powers, who retain the memory of many lives, will be called forth to aid in the lifting of the continents. Knowledge of the akasic records will aid them to inspire men less evolved.

"Continents labor to bring forth mineral life, plant life, animal life, and man's consciousness-life. Continents are used as a blanket and a canopy by the great 'Over-Lords' in the Higher Worlds who work directly with the Christ.

"Each of the seven continents has had a period of working to acquire a particular power within itself. The eighth continent is an unmanifested continent. In the measure of eternity, it is near; in the measure of man, it is millions of years ahead. This continent will upheave from the oceanic depths of the Pacific streams. The eighth continent will come into its place in the earth when the races are lifted and worships mingle. The melting pot of humanity will become the cradle for the spiritual birth of the God-men promised in all basic Scriptures.

"During the birth of the eighth continent, the earth will know great convulsions, and all continents will shift their axis points. The eighth continent is in exact alignment with the White Island—spoken of, in the Spiritual Spheres, as the Realm of the White Brothers.

"The eighth continent will contain the finest ether in its virgin soil. This ether will produce a mineral life and vegetation yet unknown to man. In the new continent men will not seek the way of the flesh in food, sex, or ambition, as they do in the present time. Men will be beyond race and religion. On this continent will live the *called-out ones,* who will be prepared for the Lord's coming. The ether in this continent will pervade and infiltrate other continents. Those who respond not to this ether, and to the Lord's time, will be isolated in a heavier ether.

"Russia has drawn to herself laggard egos out of eternity who have marched for ages on the shaded side of the pyramid. Men in Russia have accomplished the extreme opposite of the Lighted Ones who work to reach the higher peaks of evolvement.

"Russia, as a contrasting parallel, darkly opposes the rise toward Light in this planet. Since the Edenic time, nothing has been created without an opposite. Therein is the cause of struggle—and through struggle comes manifestation and birth.

"These things are beginning to be discerned by men of astute mental stature. In every age men have risen to great heights only by first being purged by the forces of the shaded ones.

"Men who take passive attitudes over a long period live in the twilight of their minds. When such men consent to the forces of evil, they come under a collective hypnosis, and follow tyrannical leaders who work for the counter-good.

"The Christ—the Rational Mind in man, and the Rational Soul in God—is never absent from the world. Regardless of how the Russian people seek to suppress the belief in God—no state-craft, order, or plan can usurp the power of God.

"The antichrist is not solely in Russia; his work may be seen in all continents. The unrest caused by the satanic inverted light touches any and all who express the desire for self-assertion and individual selfishness. This is occurring in countries and in personalities that are yet to face the Ultimates.

"The people of Russia who retain their integrity will re-embody into a continent where, by degrees, they will regain that ground which has seemingly been lost. A continent permitting brute force to enslave the many to the interest of the few will fall to a barbaric state. In Russia there will be great calamities changing the axis-pole of the continent. Russia will be iced in and under, due to a mighty cataclysmic shifting.

"India, so long a spiritual jewel in the destinies of men, will shine forth. Her progress will be of uttermost activity; her intellectual soul will come to life with the new age. India will serenely give friendship to all. Through birth, great souls will take up their abode in India. Some of these great souls once lived as historical philosophers of Greece at the height of her power.

"Many teachers have come in the last century; not all have been believed. The many interpretations of the Spiritual Worlds have confused the unknowing mind. There are some, however, with preordained hearts who recognize the working of the whole.

"Epoch-making as this time may be, it is not an abnormal time. Rejoicing, not cursing, is the order of the day.

"Steve, it is well within the plan. We of the Inner Way of life wait for you patiently. What has seemed hard to grasp shall soon be simplified to receptive minds and wills.

"Those who do most to keep alive the spiritual truths are not the brilliant intellects or the scholars or the scientists. The ones who hold the key to the spiritual truths are those who have the reverent hearts, pure minds, wisdom, and selfless wills.

"The coming mental bodies of men will see in other dimensions. When this comes, governments will not fail, because men will know and observe the law of cause and effect. When the mental body has gained a higher rate in vibration, that which has been laborious and spasmodic to man will be expressed as coordination and harmony.

"The peace of the East and the action of the West will become as one, when the purging of the now has completed its work."

These were Master R's last words to Stefan, for at this moment a revitalizing life entered into Stefan's body. As he awakened to physical consciousness, Stefan found himself being carried from the small hill where he had lain for three days.

The soul of Stefan will retain the memory of his inward experience with the Master. Henceforth, he will be one in the world who will remember that the Light is mightier than the dark.

6
Thou TiSeila

For he shall give his angels charge over thee, to keep thee in all thy ways.

—Psalm 91:11

When a disciple is entering a period of major change in his evolvement, and is preparing for a special work, certain destroying ones in the physical world come into his life. These destroying ones aid in the dissolving of old and detaining attachments, and assist the disciple in the shifting of his karmic impetus. This is known in discipleship as the *dissolution process.* However, during his period of transition, the disciple has the help of the angels and of pure persons who, as mending ones, soften the harsher blows in karma which are required in the relinquishing of certain physical attachments.

Thus, in this initiatory period of her life, Ann Ree had the help of two loving friends, who were inspired to take her to a Sierra retreat. It was here that she was to make her total linking with the powers of Mediation; here that she was to experience the Mediatory Lord of the earth—the Jesus One.

Her friends took her to Yosemite, the Great Sierras, and King's Canyon. On a beautiful day in King's Canyon, while sitting on the river bank and observing the various nature spirits in the trees and small shrubs, Ann Ree saw a vision of a Great Being walking across the water toward her. The Being was clothed in a white robe; his beard had glistening white locks. A staff was in his hand. He explained to her that he was the Venerable One or Father Jupiter; and that he worked with the Realm of Nature, the angels, and all worthy disciples. In the following days the Venerable One revealed to Ann Ree secrets of the great forests, of the redwoods; of the stones, minerals, plants; and of the sacred places in the earth where the spiritual powers may work uninterruptedly.

The scent of pines, the unpolluted streams, the rocks yet bearing the mark of the glacial times, and the fragrances of the small herbs and grasses provided a perfect background for the Venerable One's instruction. His words pertaining to the healing essence in herbs were of special interest to Ann Ree. She was told that for every bacterial sickness in the world there is an herb for its cure; and that there are antagonist herbs which heal the poisons of the mind. The Venerable One told her that physicians would return to herbal wisdom, and would minister to the bodies of men through Nature therapies, as in the time of Hippocrates. He said that men will discover unknown energies and use them in their healing therapies—particularly the energies of the sun and of the planets.

One morning while in the Great Sierras I saw before me a snake in the act of charming a bird. The bird stood paralyzed. The snake pierced him with his fangs, and opened his jaws to devour him. I was disturbed by the seeming cruelty between creatures, until the Venerable One explained to me that in Nature there is a mercy aspect in the death of creatures. The slayer is possessed by the necessity to survive, and the slain at the time of death receives a death anesthesia. This death anesthesia enables the victim to die without pain.

The Venerable One explained to me that when an animal is killed by a man, there is pain. He told me that as long as men kill animals they will also kill their fellow men.

During the harvest moon of August 1951, Ann Ree and her two beloved friends, camping at King's Canyon, witnessed in the night-sky a panorama of animals in breathtaking and awe-inspiring cloud formations—each animal a perfect cloud sculpture. They watched for a long time, in view of the full moon, as each species of the animal kingdom moved overhead in pairs across the night-sky. The animals were followed by cloud pictures of the patriarchs and the angels. Ann Ree was told inwardly that the great animal panorama is reflected through the atmosphere onto the mirrored sky every year at the time of the harvest moon; for this is the period of the year when the species-oversoul of animals reportrays itself to mankind, and renews its birth impulse into the world. The animal-species panorama may be seen, by men of pure hearts, only in the virginal places of Nature.

The three friends next visited the Sequoias. One day at dusk, while Ann Ree sat on huge Beetle Rock and contemplated the lofty trees and mountains before her, she saw the sky become completely filled with the etheric body of the Lord Jesus. The violet light of the dusk or twilight made the central note of His color.

In this contemplative time my heart united with the heart of Jesus, and I experienced His love and compassion for men of the earth. I had seen visions of Jesus many times in my life, and in these visions His words came to me in familiar Bible verses—but this was the first time He spoke to me in a personal, intimate colloquy. He told me that each day at dusk He seeks to lighten the cares of men; for the hearts of men are more responsive to His love at this time of the day.

The mighty etheric body of Jesus, in command of the earth, encompasses and saturates the earth with His love. At dusk He momentarily adjusts and modifies the burdens of the world.

One morning during my meditation, while still in Sequoia, the earth beneath my feet opened etherically and I saw underneath the seemingly secure surface many caverns of exquisite beauty. These caverns were conjoined to Beetle Rock where I had heard the voice of Jesus. Someday men will discover these caverns, and will learn that their beauty far exceeds that of the caverns now known to them.

From the time of her Easter illumination to the August days of initiation in the Great Sierras, Ann Ree experienced a rapid increase in the tempo of her telepathic alignment with the Higher Worlds. She began to receive coherent portions of beautiful prose—among these were mantrams, exquisite in their purity and composition. This was the beginning of her writing perfected mantrams, which were to come forth so voluminously. These mantrams were not only sacred word-formulas for her own spiritual emancipation, but they were also for initiates-to-be who would align themselves with the higher impulses and potencies of the Spiritual Worlds.

After her experience with Jesus in the Sequoias, there entered into Ann Ree's life direct guidance as to each step before her.

In August 1951, I made my first union with the seven centrifugal points within the medallions of the Masters—and I began to receive a composite telepathy. *In a composite telepathy the Masters do not identify themselves. A composite telepathy is made up of all the Masters speaking as one voice. I was told that henceforth I would receive from all of the Masters; for my labors had now reached the time in which I was to use the power of synthesis.*

In the beginning of the composite telepathy from the Masters, I received a series of intimate and loving passages of telepathic instruction. These personal telepathic passages became the balm to heal the torturous wounds of the past years, and they prepared me for the coming labors. During this special interval of healing closeness with the Masters, I lived in uttermost quiet and spiritual serenity. Their love for me and their insight into my soul gave me a re-evaluation of myself, and also made clear to me the necessity of using my gifts to help and to heal in the world.

When the Masters sent their composite telepathy to Ann Ree, they would reveal their presence and begin their instruction with the words, "Thou TiSeila"—using her name from a past life in which she had used initiate powers in Atlantis. The following passages are from the composite telepathy received by Ann Ree between August and December 1951.

Sequoia Forest, California
August 11, 1951

Thou TiSeila,

Beloved daughter out of the far days, not too much time is allotted thee. Therefore, treasure the jewel given thee of the now, and fret not. Remember when our Lady appeared to thee in the vision of the past, and comforted thee with the words: "Fret not thyself because of evildoers."

Thou hast been shown that even the most solid mountain is attainable to thee. In these rich latter days for thee, as the purging grows more fiery and the pain more intense, a body of beauty in likeness to Light is being created.

It is much to ask of the lion meekness, patience. But even as the harvest is nigh and the grapes are ripening on the vine, so will the overflowing heart's love fill to the full the chalice of thy last days.

The first vow is, "No harmful word regarding any one or any thing for all time"—a strong vow to take, and not required of shallow minds. The victory over speech removes the last barrier to the thrones of Heaven.

Thou now makest thy second vow. "Define

for thyself, 'What *is* the way?'" Live each moment as the design harmonious to thy soul's seeking. The instrument is not the server until he hath equipped himself with a shoulder for heavier labors.

Over a virgin hill the archetype which hath been quickened for thee awaiteth thee—for which thou canst truly be joyful.

Daughter, claim thy family! Be as the eagles. Live with the angelic thoughts. Be godlike in thy dignity, but sweet and gracious in thy spirit.

Take on the body of *Light*. Dwell not upon the corruption of those who sought to pollute thee. Corruption and Heaven are far apart.

On this mountain height, thou hast experienced more, far more than thy innermost soul knoweth. This virginal place is in complete rapport with, and in exact dimension to, a mighty Royal Power Sphere.

In thy receivings and recordings, remember no two express alike in the world of judgments, and no two enter the gate alike in spiritual respondings. But all eventually will fulfill the day of their evolving proportions, for in the coming ether-time of the earth, men will respond to one another even as the stars and Hierarchs now work as one.

As thou goest down into the valley, report to thy heart that all is well, that no further demands will be made in thy mind as to what thy heart needeth. For the rest of the way is the heart-way—and as thou knowest now faintly, thou wilt come to know strongly, the Christ-way.

*

Santa Barbara, California
September 12, 1951

Thou TiSeila,

Daughter in the Christed Light, let thy mending include reality as to man's place in the earth. Learn that the many particles of man record the frail and also the good. Concern thyself with the walk upward unto God.

In thy younger days, life, as a ball of string, was rolled toward thee. Now thine own cord of soul-reaching hath the reverse in action, for from thee must the golden cord be untwined.

Make thy holy recollections as the hands on the thread, as thou spinnest out of thyself the recallings of pain and of glory. Praise even those threads which have given thee bondage, but in reality were thy soul's anchor to the earth.

Sing at thy work, and others soon shall join in the song. Thy loom groweth wide; thy arm and hand dextrous. Let it not be said others weaved and thou didst wait.

Weave well at thy work; shine with joy in the craft-beauty at hand. So light the way each day. Reflect on the cord—hath it spun well?

Daughter of the olden days, be diligent with thy time. Around thee are the friendly faces and kindly hands who aid thee in the task of reclaiming the old into the new.

Where the sun falleth into shadow, cling not; turn to thy weaving again, though the thread beareth the salt of thy tears.

Daughter, thou art of the moon's wistfulness and of the sun's fire. Shut not out thy light.

*

Santa Barbara, California
September 29, 1951

Thou TiSeila,

Now daughter, dost thou think that thoughts are unheard, unrevealed?

What are fears, but the shadows in an empty house of many rooms, in which one roams to drabber states, to aimlessness?

Let not the wound, from which the blood hath ceased to flow, pain thee. God hath sounded to thee in the far off days; and He soundeth to thee in the days of the now.

Even as the sun falleth on the shaded trees, so shineth the Christed Sun to thee and on thee. The white Light of the Christ giveth to thy spirit iron, steel, diamond, gold—and lastly, thine own rosy soul-tone.

Take thy measure through a requited mind and spirit, and thou shalt receive the whole in fulfillment.

Daughter, thou art beloved—and the beloved are never lost. Draw thy shield about thee. Be golden in thy light once again.

It is now a fair day for the kindling of the spirit, and for the lighting of the heart's fire. Let thy light burn upon the heights to light the far-away ones. Let the glowing love of thy heart's flame cleanse thy desirings.

That day which is in Christ hath come unto thee; and thy soul resteth well as the words of the Christ are heard in thy heart's ear. Michael hath placed his shield upon thee and hath called thee to the army of the Christed ones.

And now of love, make not terms with thy receiving. Be in the dawn even as in the dusk. If that which thou lovest be as the serpent to thee, then send it back unto the desert-way.

Let joy and laughing return. Let the golden light sift in softly to thy sight. Let it cover all thou seest.

Meet with fortitude the lion who on uncertain ground devoureth what standeth innocently before him. Falter not, if evil glance on thee; let him gaze, but stand thou firm. Thou art encased in thy soul's virtue. The *last* lion standeth now before thee; hunt thou not in confining places, but keep thy vision open to that which is nigh and also far to thee.

Thou shalt not hear the bell summoning thee till thou hast cleared the way. For it is a joyful valley in which thou shalt work—a harmony of sharing in song. One hill now remaineth between thee and the tolling of the sound which ringeth only to the rhythm of the heart's higher and hidden beat.

Go forth; love; will; work to this end; serve within the treasure archives in God. If the thunder of another way rolleth about thee, proceed on thy way. The passage is ahead; it is also nigh and by thee, not afar.

*

Refugio Pass, California
September 30, 1951

Thou TiSeila,

Let the space places be thy home and house. Let thy gaze be as the cloud-changer. Let thy desires go forth to new abodes each day. In this, thy vision will remain upon that which thou workest.

In the olden days men dwelt in small hutments with vast places and grand view-points. Today, in larger lodgings, men increase wrong discernings. Let properties be naught to thee but to support that spoken of as the Real.

Earth is filled with men who live in the corruption of their own smotherings.

Blessed one of ancient days, thou hast only to mix the mortar with the sacred stones. Thou hast only to fire thy hearth with the fire of constant love—and lo, it is Christ who bringeth forth the bread, that He may give to the many who hunger and want.

Let not thy light keep watch over ruins of wasted places. Light thy face to better see the face of thy brother's child who crieth in the night, calling to thee in fear of separateness.

Daily make preparation, but cloud not thy vision with plan in creation. Creation hath long been set to scope and pattern. Creation's revealings may be read, if in thy soul thou keepest the striving true.

Keep at thy small tasks, which oft seem as dunes of sand; yet keep diligently the duty nigh to thy gaze, as thou wouldst keep thy sheep or thy cattle grazing in greener, wider places.

Dost thou not remember?—thou hast the secret formula of the days, and also of the yonder in place.

Make resolute thy plan to live within the Plan. Thou hast been conceived in the eternals. Believe on thy soul's work as if thou wert the one keeper of the one-light, yet knowing ever that thou art not alone at thy task.

*

Lompoc Lagoon, California
September 30, 1951

Thou TiSeila,

Thou standest on the bridge between earth and Heaven—the bridge spanning the old of the past and the new in the Christ.

As on that great day when the sun was set for an earth to follow, so did the Christ touch the earth, that He might replace with Light that which moved as darkness in the deep.

Let thy heart be in deep earnestness, devoting thy ways as a continued testimony to Light.

Let love be thy horizon's bow-cloud—and the shining radiance of thy spirit will come forth rosy as the peach, and golden as the sacred fire.

Thou turnest to the Ancient Ones who dwelt with thee in the former TiSeila days.

Go to the olden stone—the core of heat in life—and learn to walk through the encentered fire of the earth. Make then thy climb to the Christ from plane to plane; for most sacred are the ways of God in earth, and most sacred are comparisons with Heaven. Learn of these, and thou shalt set the pendulum in thy heart to rest.

TiSeila, there is a Hierarch difference between keeping alert and keeping abreast with the time-happenings in the now. That which is alert is instinctual, and that which keepeth abreast is co-working and coherent in Christ.

Thine olden name "TiSeila"—which hath now claimed thee—is thy soul-call name. The name "Clisome" is thy initiate-name, and meaneth initiate of sun and moon. TiSeila revealeth the records of the day of the deep, and remaineth with thee until the earth becometh a star.

True naming is the work of the ages or aeonic days. When one receiveth the recordings of the true name, he holdeth the golden arterial thread which never breaketh nor is broken asunder from Him who sent it out.

How long hast thou sought thy name caller? Too long hast thou famished after that which is known betwixt Him and thee.

*

Santa Barbara, California
October 5, 1951

Youth, TiSeila, springeth from the free virgin impulse renewed over and over again in Him who sent thee out. The eternal in thee is malleable to the Hand of Him.

Death, TiSeila, cometh not in the stark moment of lightning's timing. But death cometh with each beat of the heart.

That which looketh on in Clisome and TiSeila seeth death and life alike—not as form in body, but as the robe put off to better sleep, to arise on the morn in fresh adornment.

Soul awake to the body alone, sleepeth to the Plan of God. Soul awake to Spirit moldeth the pattern of love for a coming morn.

Youth, TiSeila, believeth these things and wavereth not in the memory of the Father's Home.

Behold the morn. Behold the sacred bells in thy heart. The hands of men have shaped their form, but the sound of God cometh out.

Behold the temples built as shrines, where men search for a hint of the Realm of God.

Behold never death, TiSeila, but ever what Is: Life *In* God!

*

Lompoc, California
October 10, 1951

Thou TiSeila,

Thou hast now made the third vow: "The vow of the depression freeing." The sun-lit way will carry thee through the portals of time. And the crimson dusk will light the way for thy crossing over the dark of the night.

Thou art not burdened. Thou hast waded in the deep stream, and thou seemest weary; but thou hast retained the light and the good. Upon thy garments of light there lingereth the sacred odor and sanctity from that with which thou didst work.

Thou hast been given the keys to the scrolls—and the lock hangeth loose. Reverently respond to that which awaiteth recording.

Thou shalt instruct thy body, on going to sleep, to fulfill its work on the coming day. Let the night command the body powers of the day, and the risen moon command the thoughts of the light. If in the night thou hast seen sorrow over which thou hast little power, let not these shades affect thy daytime powers. Let the joy of the day roll out and build the power for the mending of men's souls.

Los Angeles, California
October 13, 1951

Thou TiSeila,

"Decision" is thy fourth vow. When sacrifice hath become not sacrifice, the authority of instantaneous decision is given to thee. That which speaketh "now or never" is the soul's timing freeing thee from karma.

Sing not a song of differences, but look for God in all persons. Let thy face look into the mirror of thyself and see the eyes of thy neighbor looking back to thee—and he is thy love.

Thy weariness, TiSeila, cometh from fear of largeness in thy labors. Thou goest forth not as a blazing light, but as the sun shining softly. As the sun cometh forth from beyond the cloud, thou comest forth again to give of thy healing, loving works.

Ask not for the small if thou wouldst walk apace in greater rhythmic goings. Thy way is the strong way. It is required of thee that thine own will shall rest within the Will of God. Courage of the past now bringeth the diamond-will to its true setting in thy heart. Thou knowest that thou goest not forth to war, but thou workest in the diamond-will.

That which is oblique worketh from below and not upon the heights. Therefore, step thou aside and let the lance touch thee not as it spendeth itself in the wind.

Dost thou think the Father's Kingdom knowest what harshness is? The thorn of Christ hath naught to do with bitterness, TiSeila. Thy loneliness is caused by the height of the mountain climb. The thorn to thee is but the last backward look onto the plane below.

Thy training over the many years beareth the marks of the Michael call. Be thou not timid—and fear not. Naught restraineth thee, save thou givest agreement.

Thy counter-tumults and recordings have now arrived onto the stream in light, and thou wilt know the joy as each burdened pawn is carried away into that great sea of swiftly moving light.

Over what, TiSeila, dost thou desire victory? Thy warrior's keynote ringeth true only to shining justice in light. Thy valor shall stand forth. Make for thyself the staunch victory. Let the shades of the day be engulfed in Knowing Light.

*

Santa Barbara, California
November 3, 1951

Thou TiSeila,

Daughter, thou knowest that when thy body doth sleep, thou art in a world where thou art at home, and where thy true nature hath full cognizance of all thou doest. On thy return to the earth thou findest it oft difficult to bring forth instruction, and the wisdom of the higher self remaineth oft silent, that earth experience may be reaped to its uttermost. Thou knowest,

TiSeila, such wisdom doth gather and increase from life to life—until thou makest a passage to bridge the deep chasm between mind and soul, and mind and body. That which cementeth the bridge and ascertaineth swiftness in flight are the vows thou dost make each night. These are the talismans for the coming day's courage and work.

Step boldly, daughter; be thou not afraid. Be thou not as the hare—thou art the lion. Be thou not small; be thou large. Give largely, and thou hast the secret of much receiving in thy walk.

Remember, thou art as a lion with a new pelt—a lion engaged in a heart-hunt. Thy hunt is the Christ as love, not the self as love.

Trust on thy spiral's climb. Mend not that which hath dried out and hath naught of mending.

Go thou now over the hill and be at peace with those who war in fear.

Let thy gentleness be as the sweet crown from which the thorn presseth no longer upon the wound.

*

Santa Barbara, California
November 6, 1951

That which is fear, TiSeila, is known as the *dearth* of the days.

Thy sendings are recorded unto those about thee. Let thy mind be not a snare unto regrettings. In thy toll to time, search for the way, and take the way of work after the skills in God. TiSeila, thy work is to serve and to call men to serve, that their hearts and minds may be free.

Thou needest not defend the Real. Do thou the good; be thou the love—and thou shalt feel naught of restraints imposed on thee. In thy heart is the light unvanquished. Grasp with all thy strength the light; and love shall be on thy lips, on thy hands.

Dost thou remember the days when thou didst see the Temple and wast given the keys? Thou hast traveled long and far, and though weary, thou art ready for the climb.

Dost thou remember when on thy hands thou didst feel the sacred words, that thy senses might reveal them to thy outer works?

Dost thou remember when thy light did hear the tones, and thou wast recalled from dead to life?

And hast thou forgotten all the years when thou didst speak, thou didst *see* all thou didst say?

Then know thou, TiSeila, thou hast long been at home; and thou art not far from peace.

*

Santa Barbara, California
November 8, 1951

TiSeila, remember, God giveth to each one in the earth the knowing of his soul's resting place. As the eagle in flight knoweth his cloud to rest upon, thy soul knoweth its place. That which beareth thy flight oft tireth thee; but that which seeketh thy cloud tireth not.

Keep thou the day in thy island of peace and love-serene, above that which destroyeth itself; for thou hast now made a covenant with Eternity.

Peace to thee is like a spear ready for battle. Thy work beholdeth thy face. That which pinioned thee to earth hath its yoke no longer upon thee. Let thy stronghold be of worth in place, time, and action.

Sleep hath perished more nations than a million avengers. Thou wast not promised the easy walk, but a walk in which the path doth grow hard. Only thy heart's light carrieth thee to thy resting place.

He who walketh swiftly seeketh not a foothold on the way. TiSeila, that which spurreth thee from the within maketh the walk—not that which driveth thee from the without. And thou hast more to tell than of the climb, TiSeila; thou tellest of the *how* in the climb. And thou tellest of the overlook which revealeth the Face of God.

Thou learnest each day the difference between the within and the Within. That which doth tell thee within is in part; and that which inspireth thee from the Within transpireth as the good—and naught upsetteth or withstandeth the good.

Thy Truth-teller, which is the Within, bringeth forth the good. Arise thou; the Within knoweth the Light.

Thy Watcher hath stood at the gate, and now he standeth before thee. Thy face no longer turneth in profile to him, but thou seest him eye to eye.

*

Santa Barbara, California
November 20, 1951

Thou TiSeila, fold thy fabrics. Put at rest thy treasures. Place them with thy earth memories which are enscrolled deep within thy heart. Thou rememberest the good, and naught of the good can be taken from thee.

Hail thou unto God; and go forth. Take thou the lance, the white banner, and thy shield. The angels go forth with thee and thine.

Because thou hast taken into this life many lives in one, there will oft be confusion in the minds of others who seek to interpret thy actions in earth.

*

Santa Barbara, California
December 4, 1951

TiSeila, a soul taketh its winged flight by habits of good. Bid thou farewell, beloved daughter, to that which hindereth by the Way. Thou art on the Way.

Thou hast escaped the coil which did enclose thee. Its mark now is thy shining light.

Make thy actions pure. Cleanse thou thy thoughts toward the work hard and long before thee. Thou hast had a story told unto thee, and thou hast been the chief actor. Let the curtain fall; and take up thy crafts behind the scenes. Prepare for thy winged soul-song portraying the Lord.

7
Andrew

Unto the upright there ariseth light in the darkness: he is gracious, and full of compassion, and righteous.

—Psalm 112:4

When Ann Ree went to California early in 1950, she left her Florida chapel in the hands of a capable student and co-worker. This friend and student, whose "grace name" was Andrew, was taken in death less than three months after she left Florida. His passing made it necessary for her to close the chapel.

Andrew had been my student for twelve years. He had a methodical mind and uttermost integrity. After my decision to return to California, I assigned Andrew to take charge of the little flock in the chapel.

Andrew conducted the Sunday morning service on the day I left for California. His service, titled "The Lady Elect," was an inspiring accolade to his teacher. His loving words were a blessing to me, for I was able to leave Florida with a free mind—knowing that the ministry had been placed in the reverent hands and devoted hearts of my students.

A month earlier Andrew had confided to me that he had a serious heart condition. As he was prepar-

ing for the Sunday service on the day of my leaving Florida, I noticed the angel-look in the pupils of his eyes. Whenever I see this look in the eyes of a person, it is telling me of his approaching death. Three months later I received the news of Andrew's death.

The innate purity and integrity of Andrew, and his conviction of a life after death, enabled him to undergo his transition into the afterlife without fear. In the three days following his death Andrew appeared to Ann Ree; and she witnessed his "glorious after-death experience."

Twenty months later, when Ann Ree was preparing to return to Florida, she began to receive thoughts transmitted telepathically from Andrew. With the aid of Master M and the White Brothers (the Men in White Apparel), Andrew was able for the first time to project sustained telepathic thought onto the screen of her mind.

He gave his viewpoint of the First Heaven, or higher astral planes, and he described the substance of the astral world as "gelatin-like." He gave her a description of ether, and told her that ether permeates and sustains all living forms. He explained to her that ether enables the cells to adhere to one another; and that ether is influenced at all times by light.

Andrew stressed the importance of prayer, and gave a detailed analysis of prayers. It was through his telepathy that Ann Ree first learned of the great Islands of Light which are built by the prayers of men. He stated that the Islands of Light make it possible for men to be more communicable to the Spiritual Worlds; and that these Islands form a light-plateau through which the Greater Beings may come closer to the needs of men. He said to her through telepathy, "The Islands of Light are used for receiving and retaining ideas given out by the Masters, so that the planetary aspects can be used to channel them to the human brain."

Andrew explained to Ann Ree that his alignment with the Masters made it possible for him to sustain his telepathic communion with her. He stated that communion with the dead is not harmful when the Great Beings help the Risen Dead to commune with their loved ones through telepathy, or the projection of pictured thoughts.

He disclosed that any form of mediumship is harmful to both the dead and the living. This explained to Ann Ree her lifelong revulsion toward any form of mediumship. She fully believed—in conformity with the Scriptures—that men endanger themselves when they deliberately recall the dead from their labors, or trespass into the world of the dead with selfish motives or intent.

There was never any question in my mind as to life after death. I knew that the dead lived; and that there were many phases of the after-death state. However, my training had taught me to avoid deliberate communion with the dead. My research into the world of the dead had been through dreams and through reassuring telepathies. When Andrew held ajar the door for my research into the world of the dead, I knew that I had reached the point in my evolvement where I must look more deeply into the world of the dead—

so that I might qualify myself to be initiated into more extensive revelations regarding Heaven.

Andrew's telepathic communion with Ann Ree continued from November 15 to December 2, 1951. The following passages are the thoughts he projected to her during this period:

> I have been under the instruction of the White Brothers (Men in White Apparel). The Brother says it is not easy to receive the different wave lengths between the two worlds. He says it is on too high a frequency here; and that an instrument like yourself receives in flashes. So we "can" it up, as you did on the recorder. Then you receive it as a telepathy in story form.
>
> The things here in the Inner Planes are the other side of what you see. You are in a karmic reflecting plane.
>
> Since I left the earth, I have been working on these ideas: the truth must be told, or silence kept; the feelings must be kept calm in all conditions; be an observer and an actor; extreme prudence; extreme fidelity; extreme loyalty; extreme patience; extreme consecration.
>
> Women *are* different instruments. But the Brothers do not see them as unreliable instruments. They look on them as having more lasting healing powers.
>
> Not many men or women have access to the akasic records; the karma and the sacrifice are greater for those who do. This is why women as receivers must never lose sight of harmony

within all, for they must work against a collective instinct. To have equal or androgynous polarity imposes great demands, and more is asked of the woman in her spiritual work.

In your classes we spoke so much of the planets and their effect on men's lives. The planets affect these planes in a very different way from the way they affect the earth. The Greater Beings, working with the energies of the planets, direct human karma. Whatever man builds into his mental body, the planets record here in a belt of reflecting light. This builds what is called the earth's mental body, which influences the future mental bodies of men to be born on earth.

Every one born on the earth planet is gravity-bound, whether he lives for the physical life or the spiritual life. All on earth are bound to the same system. The earth is a sphere of karma responding to the tone of karma in a Universal Scheme.

As you so often said in our teaching, "We are all creators." It is the earth we are working with.

Six of the Masters have been freed from the karmic gravity set up in the earth's system; they now work with the Over-Lords of universal addition (equation). A seventh will soon join them.

When one is in the astral world, he cannot see the earth, but he can sense what is going on in the earth. If one receives training before death, this becomes a life-thread or line between the astral world and the physical world.

The Masters' telepathy forms a small world of light. When I want to contact your thoughts, I am attracted to this small world of light. Then with the help of the Brothers, and the prayers of the living and the dead, I can send you my thoughts—though you do not always receive them in the same timing. It depends on your frame of mind.

I can best describe what the Higher World compares with by using this example. The earth is a cup. The astral world and the life in it are the handles of the cup. The Overdirecting Intelligence, or the Father, holds the cup. That which is in the cup is mind.

The higher astral planes are to the Spiritual World what air is to the earth world. The ethers in the higher astral planes make it possible for men to mediate between Spirit and matter. Since the higher astral planes are the meeting places between soul and Spirit, they are the means by which soul carries out the formulas between body and Spirit. Jacob's ladder in the Bible is an illustration of the actual experience of penetrating the higher astral planes to reach the Spiritual Realms beyond.

To avoid the word "astral" is to not receive the full value of its ways and works. To say it is the place of "desire" takes in only certain actions. The word "astral" means Planet Light; it is the reflection from Planet Light that makes the astral world. If there were no moon or sun, or Mars, Mercury, Saturn, etc., there would be only astral latency, not action.

When any spiritual work is done, it is done not *in* the astral world, but *because* of the astral world. The astral world is merely the pillar supporting the spiritual archetypal formulas and forms.

Where the Bible speaks in Genesis of the firmament, it is speaking of the astral world. It was from the firmament (astral world) that the planets were sent forth. The energies of the planets are reflected into the astral world. These energies influence the actions of men.

To some, until a certain stamina is gained after death, everything is enlarged or malshaped, looking something like a magnifying mirror's enlarging and distorting. During the first ninety days after death the astral world is not understood at all. There is a certain work done on the body left off—and a mending done on the body left on; then the forms around one begin to take shape with extended meaning. Thus, each thing becomes self-explanatory as one sees it.

The Source of things, as far as I can as yet see, is of such brilliant Light it can only be understood in portions of experiences. These experiences give stamina to the vehicle worn after death.

The law of gravity in the physical world works upon the physical body and the lesser etheric body. In the astral world, the law of gravity works in the thought. The gravity in the astral world, working with the sun and the moon, forms a cleansing matrix. All are drawn into this matrix after death so that the pain shell (lesser emotional body) may be cast aside. Sensation cannot reach into the higher levels of the astral light. Pain is the highest expression of sensation, contrary to the generally accepted idea that joy is the highest.

What is really joyous over here works through the highest astral-light material, with the aid of the angels. It is only reached by man on earth, or out of earth, by his striking a tone in creation which is a totally perfect part of the Source in Creation. Those on earth closest to the Father are the ones who are doing His work out of a purity within their own soul-grace.

As it is taught, there are seven steps or parts to each plane in the astral world. The four lower parts of each plane retain the earth reflection, and the three upper parts of the plane express, in some degree, the light from Heaven.

The student of the "inner meaning within" is so confused over the many interpretations of the astral world that he ignores its importance to his spiritual life on earth; he overlooks the fact that he is never out of the astral world. The astral world is the first world we are trained in when the earth body is put aside. The etheric body is the body for momentum in the physical world; the body for equilibrium in the astral world; and the body for poise of the soul.

In our karmic turn-back we are put in the place of those we have hurt. After death, while pain and earth-passion still cling to the pain shell, many things of a revolting and unhappy nature may be seen here. This is the place where things are taught by direct example, with feeling fully shared by looking on at the suffering of others. This is a purgatorial experience and the means by which karmic detachment is reached before we can go on to higher regions to work.

This can be experienced, while still on earth, by dream visits or night flight. When this occurs, karma is being speeded up in both worlds—preparing one for some specializing soul-process.

Time in the Inner World is something I wondered about while on earth. But I understand from the Brother that Time is a mercy agent in the law of karma. Were it not for Time men would be overcome in the overloads of force and pressures. Time is a regulating providence, giving men their chance to make their world at one with the World of God.

The astral world is filled with planes of correspondences. That which is bacteria on earth has an exact corresponding correlative in the astral life as thought. When great epidemics occur on earth, it is because mass thought has gotten out of order. The metaphysicians of the earth should first define the streams of thought alien to health. 

Nothing physical ever completely heals the physical body. Healing first takes place in the mind, working through thought correspondences by faith. If the thought causing sickness is etched in from other lives, this sometimes requires many lives to set it aright. A so-called incurable disease is a cell imbalanced by a bacterial agent out of tune with its thought correspondence in the astral world.

All men are subjected to change. The Ultimates exist in the World of God. When man discovers and relates himself to the seven Ultimates, he is then working in harmony with God, and the result is of good.

The physical world with its constant state of change exercises the soul-powers into faculties for the use of the world.

The saying of the Lord Jesus to "be of good cheer" is the outer cardinal expectancy of one spiritual Ultimate. The Lord Jesus gave the seven great Ultimates. When the Light of the Christ shines into the earth body, there is a great responding in all the planes from earth to Heaven.

Even as in the physical, there are no vacuums in the astral world; however, the reaction to things is quicker in the astral than in the physical world. When one thing is removed, another immediately takes its place (always according to the order of what it replaces—its part or its replica). It is in the power of thought to replace an inferior thought with a superior thought in the range of consciousness.

A cheering mind, a cheerful thought, keeps the level of creation on the level of the Brothers' work in Christ. This is sustained by unselfish thoughts. Unselfish thoughts work with the Ultimates, which are instantaneous in their active principles.

A lukewarm view of the spiritual life is harmful. It fails in the rhythm of activity in creation—and a biased thing is created in the thought. This becomes a partly concave formation, and is more belligerent than the strongest particle thrown by deliberation. There are astral walls surrounding people possessing such views. These walls dissolve only from inner pain. Pain is fire. When the astral walls are consumed by the fire of pain, the Presences in Light can come forth to help.

In the life after death, something of this kind happens too, but it is not quite the same—for walls of bias and prejudice are spiral-like in the astral world; and we meet them one at a time. In the earth, the walls of bias and prejudice fall "as the walls of Jericho." Few are prepared for the exposure of their sensibilities to the downpouring of light shed on them—and an initiation occurs. At this moment the one on earth begins the work of his soul.

When men think of the astral world as an indefinable mystery, this becomes an obstruction rather than a help in their spiritual research on earth and after death.

As to size, shape, range, and place of the astral world: it encircles and interpenetrates every part of the physical world. Particularly is its action parallel to the central core of the earth, where it gathers a momentum to work with the etheric substance required for a more pliant action in astral-form pageantry. If it were not for this work, men would not receive symbols in their dreams and in their visions.

Ether is a coagulating agent in the astral world, even as it is in the blood of man—for ether is the mingling fiat. Ether is chameleon-like, in that the quality of ether is determined by that which it adheres to, lives in, and of. Ether has the power to transform the coarsest matter into the finest waves of energy within light. It is the means of retaining the living substance of Spirit on any plane—from matter to Spirit. It is the substance making possible the intermingling of all substances; and action within all realms, spheres, planes—objective and subjective.

If it were not for the ether accompaniment to the working of the astral world, that which is astral would result in a frozen or static substance. The astral world would be an enlarged abnormality attached to our earth world. Ether keeps movement, clarity, and geometric precision exact. Ether coordinates that which is supple in all planes. The study of ether's work will extend the range of symbolic patterns, enabling them to become an actuality to the rational mind. When one understands the transforming pliability of ether, and relates himself to the law of cause and effect, he can accomplish miracles as to precision and timing.

When ritual is recollected by the soul-power, and is orally used, ether becomes a directing and controlling agent in the astral world. Ritual uses ether to unfold the formulas supporting the functions of the soul.

In the world of earth and materiality, habits good or bad respond to the function of ritual used by the higher mind. Habits built by repetition unconsciously use ether to create the coarser manifestations within the world of outer form.

What is set down so clearly in the Scrolls of the Archetypes is filtered down with the aid of the Great Archangel Beings. Men on earth receive the Archetypal Scrolls when they are ready to enter a new phase of evolvement. During these periods prayers change and become more intense in their rhythms; they are charged with a vibrancy of up-going life, in preparation to meet the wisdom of the greater spirals in light. There seems to gather, with the sea of upcoming prayers, a universal desire for the good of all men.

I am told that, as man becomes more of a spiritual identity, the soul impulse comes closer to the original plan in God.

Andrew's telepathies ceased on December 2, 1951.

In the year of 1926, long before she met Andrew, Ann Ree had painted the portrait of a man unknown to her. With the painting came these words in light, "Dearest friend and protector." In the year of 1950, while looking through her files, she came upon this old portrait—and recognized it to be the face of Andrew.

Andrew was of an austere and esthetic nature. Like many male initiates he had yet to define woman's place in the spiritual life. Therefore, it is interesting to see that in his first telepathic words to me he mentioned woman's place in a spiritual life.

When Andrew was living, we had many conversations pertaining to woman and her physical and spiritual place in the world. I explained to him that women who have attained the higher spiritual initiations use the androgynous powers of their souls; and should be looked upon as fellow disciples.

In the present age there is a matriarchal emphasis upon spiritual evolvement. Thus, the feminine disciple finds it more natural to fulfill the spiritual life. The majority of men are more religiously than spiritually inclined and, therefore, are least found in spiritual environments.

If a male initiate has any remaining traits of masculine vanity, he often questions why he finds few men in spiritual groups. If he is unwilling to relinquish his vanity and to receive instruction, his soul directs him into situations wherein he will gain more sympathetic rapport with the feminine principle. Should he turn a deaf ear to the signal from his soul—and desire worldly approval—he will miss his spiritual opportunity. Thereafter, he is led into worldly and sentient traps, until his sense of values comes to balance with the timing of his soul.

The male initiate who fulfills a spiritual life—having developed in previous lives an inward harmony as to the masculine and feminine attributes within himself—sees all relationships in the highest light, and feels no barrier to association with his fellow disciples be they male or female.

Because this is a materialistic age, the male initiate is more often criticised for his spiritual aspiration than is the feminine initiate. His trials are heavier in that minor and major temptations press against him from every side. The male initiate who takes a stand for his spiritual life shall be protected and sustained by the Spiritual Worlds; and he shall be morally and physically rewarded, and fruitfully compensated as to his personal well-being.

The greatest danger in the life of the male initiate is that he become smug in his beliefs; or feel that he has "arrived"; or that he is exempt from the trials which all men and women must undergo to attain spiritual power.

In the present age the pure male initiate is a rar-

ity—for the pressures of the world present greater initiatory trials than have ever been known to the male who would dedicate and devote himself to a spiritual life.

Jesus called Nicodemus a "master of Israel" because Nicodemus was a traditional initiate of Israel. Moses was an accredited initiate of the Egyptian schools. In all ages there have been different initiatory schools and branches of initiation. In the time of Greece there were the Pythagorean initiatory schools. In the virginal period of Egypt there were first the Osiris, and then the Isis schools of initiation. In the darkened Ammon period of Egypt, initiation was degraded to psychical initiatory rites of black occultism. In Babylon, previous to the time of Abraham, there were initiatory schools bordering on the sciences. In Persia there were initiatory schools relating to rituals of magic. In India and China there were no formal initiatory schools—one was instructed by a direct teacher—in China, by a philosopher; in India, by a guru. Since the coming of Jesus, the initiatory schools of the invisible and heavenly worlds have been open to the worthy ones living in the physical world.

In December 1951, Ann Ree returned to Florida, where she began to receive a downpouring of illuminative manuscript from the composite telepathy of the Masters. Each evening the visions and ideas, like "golden hail from Heaven," came so rapidly that it was impossible for her to write down all she saw, heard, and experienced. A friend and student, Eleanor "Liebschien" Muusmann, endeavored to take her dictation, but they both realized that further assistance would be necessary. When Ann Ree wondered about the help that was promised to her regarding the manuscript, she was shown a vision of a young man standing over some office equipment. The vision was accompanied by the words, "Even now one knocketh at the gate— one J.M., who cometh to share the load."

8
Barjona Days

Let a man so account of us, as of the ministers of Christ, and stewards of the mysteries of God.

—I Corinthians 4:1

A crisis in the life of an individual achieves its design and purpose when it is the means of prompting him to turn to God. Therefore, a crisis is sometimes the prelude to a more reverent and spiritual life. As the shadow of crisis is replaced by the light of new vision, one rejoices with words similar to those of the Psalmist who said, "It is good for me that I have been afflicted; that I might learn Thy statutes" (Psalm 119:71).

Late one evening in February 1952, a distraught young man came to Ann Ree's home and asked if he might see her. She intuited instantly the urgency of his need and—even though the hour was late—consented to see him. After a long discussion which lasted into the deep hours of the night, the young man was comforted. He left her presence feeling that a great burden had been lifted from him. A few weeks later he visited Ann Ree again—this time, to thank her for her help and midnight counsel. At the end of their conversation, she placed several philosophical and historical books into his hands. Thus began the association between Ann Ree and her future assistant.

There were many in my life who were a blessing and a joy to me. However, before Jonathan Murro came into my life, I had yet to earn a dedicated co-worker. Those who assisted me were interested only in what my prophetic gifts could do for them personally; or they retained certain reservations due to their religious or social status. Jonathan was the first person to be concerned with the world-need and what my work could do for the world; and he gave himself without reservation. He literally catapulted himself into the work—and accepted, without question, every phase of the work. With wisdom beyond his years, he saw my potential—but more, he saw the necessity to instruct men in living truths.

When Jonathan first came into my life, he had had no religious training or preparation; however, he had a spiritual heart and soul. Even though young in years, he was weary of worldly compromises. He desired more than anything to live a clean, pure, ethical life; and he had an asset more valuable than all things—that is, an intuitive heart which knew and recognized truth.

I had long been accustomed to persons who doubted my veracity; or who sought to exploit me; or who were indifferent; or who believed in me for their own interests. Therefore, Jonathan's total acceptance of my words and works was, to me, a holy miracle. Through my catalyst association with him, I was at last free to articulate my visions. God had sent me the one who would support the structure of my labors.

My first meeting with Ann Ree took place in St. Petersburg, Florida, in December 1951. I had learned about her several months earlier from some business associates who told me of the important role she had played in their lives. These friends were among the few persons who knew of her quiet return to Florida after an absence of almost two years. They alerted me to her arrival in the city, and suggested that I contact her.

When I introduced myself to Ann Ree, I remarked how much her daughter Harriette resembled her. (The first time I saw Harriette, the sister-in-law of one of my friends, a light was around her. Now I saw that same light around her mother.)

As Ann Ree spoke, I began to see why others had been so enthusiastic in their praise of her. Within a short period of time my immediate questions were answered; and as I left her study, I promised myself that I would visit her again.

Several weeks later we had our second meeting. After our conversation I felt encouraged and inspired—and I marvelled at her graciousness and magnanimity.

When I met Ann Ree I was twenty-four years old; my time was being divided between a baseball career and the real estate business. A recurrent knee injury was forcing me to discontinue professional baseball; and, even though I was successful as a realtor, I was beginning to lose interest in real estate as a profession.

One evening in February 1952, a rapid succession of personal and business crises reached a climax. For the first time in my life, I found myself bewildered and alone. I tried to think of someone who could help me, but at first I could think of no one. Then, the name Ann Ree Colton came to my mind. Recalling our two previous conversations, I felt certain that she was the one to whom I could turn for help.

When I went to her residence, a nurse answered the door and told me that Ann Ree was not well. "Liebschien" Muusmann, the nurse who answered the door, recalls the night of this visit: "The young man who stood before me at the door seemed to be in urgent need. I said to Ann Ree, who at the time was recovering from pneumonia and laryngitis, 'There is a very distressed young man at the door. Do you think you are able to talk to him?' She sat up suddenly and said, 'Show him in. I've been expecting him since early afternoon'."

Liebschien returned to me, saying, "Mrs. Colton will have to remain in bed while she sees you. And her voice will be very weak, due to her recent illness."

Ann Ree, accustomed to unusual emergencies, greeted me with a barely audible, "Good evening."

While I spoke about the circumstances leading up to my visit, she shook her head slowly from side to side; and several times repeated the word "karma." I did not know what the word meant, but it seemed to describe how I was feeling.

It was well after midnight when I departed. Although I did not realize it at the time, the storm of disturbing events had thrust me across the threshold of a new life.

As soon as I learned that Ann Ree was well again, I went to her home to thank her for her kindness and help. Before I left, she handed me several books—one being a philosophical textbook. It was in this book that I first learned of the law of karma and the law of reincarnation. When I returned the books we discussed their contents, and she was able to explain how the laws of karma and reincarnation were working in my life. I told her that I thought the textbook was cold in its intellectual approach to these subjects—and that it lacked love. I saw that this observation pleased her.

Thereafter, each Saturday morning at ten o'clock I visited Ann Ree and received my first training in meditation. I soon learned some of the reasons why the daily practice of meditation is spiritually rewarding. The quiet of meditation becomes as a wellspring of peace, to which one may turn for renewal and refreshing; sometimes, meditation acquaints one with the world of visions.

One evening, while I was quietly meditating, a beautiful white rose appeared before me in a vision. The rose was in an exquisite and unusually designed chalice. When I told Ann Ree about the vision, she interpreted the symbology for me. (Her knowledge of symbology—which she has been acquiring since early childhood—is invaluable to her students; for she is able to explain their puzzling dreams and visions.)

Saturday morning meditation counsel with Ann Ree was to me a most precious time. We achieved a rapport in our association which enabled her to recover several of my past-life records. These were recorded in dramatic story-like form.

It was revealed to her that I had lived as an artist in the sixteenth century. A short time later, while I was visiting an art center in Clearwater, Florida, I saw the name of this artist on a volume in the library. The volume contained several of his paintings, one of which was a self-portrait. When I saw the face of the artist I was astonished—for it was my own face! This was my first literal proof of the law of re-embodiment. From this and other experiences, I learned that it is not unusual for a person to retain a similarity in features from former lives.

History took on a new and exciting meaning when I related myself, through my own previous lives, to the different periods and events in the earth's past.

Further research into other of my past-life records revealed that Ann Ree and I had known each other and had worked together many times in former lives.

I began to look forward to her weekly classes, and Sunday sanctuary services. It was in the sanctuary that I received my first true glimpse of her spiritual power and of her tall stature as a servant of God. When I noticed that her beautiful words were not being recorded, I offered to record and type her sanctuary services and classes. I learned that she did not prepare her talks, but always spoke inspirationally. This made me even more determined to preserve her words so that others might share in their beauty and receive their blessing.

The following mantram, one of her first "Angel-to-Angel Mantrams," was spoken spontaneously during a Sunday worship service:

Beloved one, my angel speaks to your angel.
There is no separation.
Wherever you are,

And whatever is given unto you,
My love sends to you impersonally
The gift of my heart after God.
Let our souls sing with joy,
Recalling the memory of what has been.
And let our eyes see, in the upperlook,
That which is to come to us
Through the Love of God.
Beloved, my angel speaks to your angel,
And asks that the healing come unto thee.
My soul speaks to your soul,
Knowing that all is well
Between Christ and thee
And Christ and me.

Ann Ree reserved one room in her home for a meditation sanctuary. This room contained an altar with fresh flowers, and on the walls were several of her paintings. Plain white candles burned upon the altar. No incense was used; for she believed that incense built an occult rather than a spiritual atmosphere. Twenty-five to forty people assembled in the sanctuary each Sunday morning.

One Sunday, after worship service, I was asked to extinguish the flame of a candle used during the service. In a careless, matter-of-fact manner, I blew on the flame; but it remained burning. The second time I blew much harder; but the flame did not flicker and continued to burn brightly. The flame finally responded to my third attempt.

When I mentioned this to Ann Ree, she said, "Any object on the altar becomes animated by the transcendent power of the Spirit during worship. Candlelight is particularly receptive to the light of Heaven. The angel who watches over the inner flame of the candle used in worship will bestow a blessing upon the one who reverently extinguishes the flame."

This was my first concrete lesson in reverence—and I knew that I had received a blessing from a Superior World.

In my association with Ann Ree I learned that nothing in human action is wasted after one opens his mind and heart to deeper spiritual instruction. A vivid lesson in this occurred when my daily meditation began to be disturbed by the memory of a business transaction in which I had participated three years earlier. The memory of this transaction continued to enter my mind—interfering with the peace necessary for meditation.

When one of the parties connected with the transaction telephoned Ann Ree and asked for an appointment, I recognized the call to be more than a coincidence. The woman who called had been the seller in the transaction—and I knew that I must contact her immediately. During the course of our telephone conversation, I learned that the woman had made a last-minute reduction in price to the purchaser of her property, but had neglected to notify me. I told her that the reduction meant she had made a slight overpayment to me, and that I would like to send her a check for the difference.

After settling this matter, the memory of the business transaction no longer interfered with my meditation. I realized that the guidance I had received during

Akasic Records of Lemuria. Painted by Ann Ree in 1925. This painting opened to her the story of Lemuria.

The Deluge, painted in 1926, initiated Ann Ree into Atlantean knowledge.

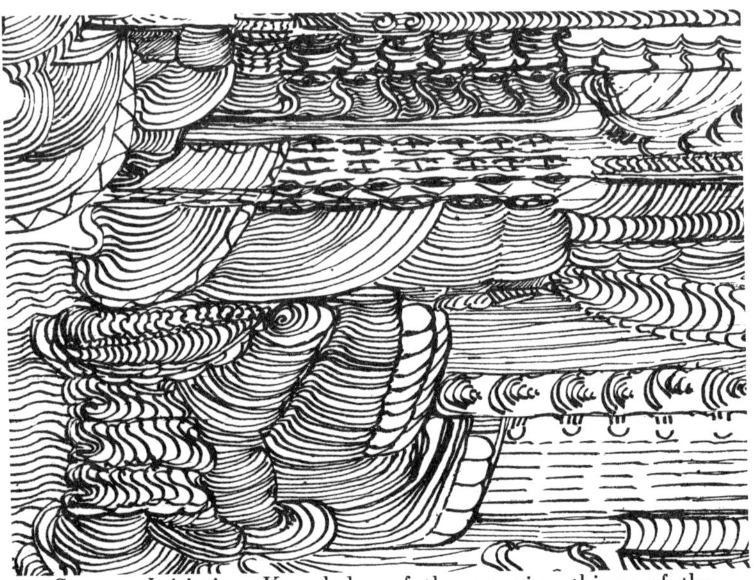

Serpent Initiation. Knowledge of the creeping things of the earth was incorporated into Ann Ree's memory and thoughts. Painted in 1926.

Astrological Akasic Record of A.R.C. Drawn by her in 1929, after receiving night instruction in etheric astronomy.

Kabalistic painting, titled *Music.* The Music of the Spheres became audible to Ann Ree through this painting (1923).

Kabalistic painting, *Christ is Risen.* Painted during Easter, 1930.

1944.

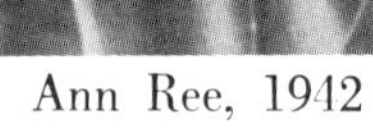

Ann Ree, 1942

In the chapel in Florida, 1950.

meditation was valid; and that the deeper recesses of my mind had projected to the surface of my consciousness the stumbling block to my practice of meditation. Added to this was my participation in the woman's joy in receiving money desperately needed at that time; for she had recently sent forth a prayer for funds to help toward her daughter's tuition and entry into college.

This experience was a lucid example of the law of equation or balance. It convinced me that each person is given the opportunity to correct the errors committed wittingly or unwittingly. Ann Ree told me that I was in the process of "making the balance or making aright anything left undone." She said, "The disciple is always given the opportunity to set aright any imbalance in the immediate and resolvable karma. All seeming coincidences are supported by immutable laws."

Two years later the woman in the business transaction, Mrs. K., visited Ann Ree on Easter Sunday. For many years she had loved and respected Ann Ree, whom she called "a saint." Mrs. K. was overjoyed when she learned for the first time that I was associated with her beloved friend and advisor. She spoke informally and voluntarily to those still present after the Easter service, and told of having known Ann Ree over the years. She described Ann Ree's ministry; its problems and persecutions; and its acceptance, finally, by the city.

Ann Ree and I discovered that we had other mutual friends and acquaintances. Among these was an elderly lawyer, who was one of the most beloved men in Florida. This noble man proved to be an inspiration to us both through his love and faith; his advice and counsel were invaluable to us. He sometimes called Ann Ree an "angel-evangelist."

Ann Ree called her home "Barjona" in memory of Alma Jones, whom she thought of as a "Peter disciple." Barjona was a happy, busy place—a spiritual home. Almost all who came to visit Ann Ree were filled with questions which had been unanswered by their former training in religion and metaphysics. Whenever someone asked her a question pertaining to spiritual matters, the question ignited her illuminative vision, and she immediately received the answer.

All who attended dusk meditation at Barjona were invited to remain for the evening meal. When an invitation was extended to me, I wondered about her "vegetarian meals," for I did not see how anyone could live without eating meat. I was surprised to find a large variety of foods, including many different types of appetizing and satisfying dishes. I found myself looking forward to these interesting dinners, which were always accompanied by a great deal of wit, as well as serious discussions about current events, philosophy, foods, astrology, astronomy, Christianity, and a number of other subjects.

At Barjona there was always a happy, festive feeling during dinner. Mealtime was a true agape—and a spiritual emanation spread among all who were present.

One evening I had dinner in a local cafeteria, and the food caused me to become nauseated and sick. When I recovered, I found that I no longer desired meat of any kind.

When a disciple begins to meditate, he is brought

face to face with certain laws of renunciation. In some instances he desires to refrain from eating meat.

Many persons who cross my path are vegetarians; each feels that he has found the exact procedure and formula for a vegetarian diet. These persons have found their own selective-palate level, and thus are nourished and contented.

A total vegetarian diet has a purifying and cleansing effect; however, if a person is untrained as to nutrition, he can upset the balance of his body chemistry. A person should not undertake a vegetarian diet until he understands the laws of nutritional balance.

The first requirement for the spiritual disciple is self-control. When a postulant-vegetarian has any lingering sensuousness of the palate, his intellect might be satisfied as to his diet, but he has yet to sublimate his sensuous palate; and he often appeases his cravings by indulging in ice cream, sweets and rich desserts.

I have seen repeatedly that persons with occult or psychic tendencies who fanatically observe a vegetarian diet, and also adhere to long periods of fasting, become psychically erratic.

The Western disciple is born to a world of competition. A vegetarian diet will soften his worldly aggressive tendencies. However—if he has failed to sublimate his competitive drives—a vegetarian diet, rather than lessening his competitive drives, will accentuate them: he becomes fanatical as to food; and vegetarianism becomes his religion.

An extreme vegetarian diet without protein fails to nourish the ancestral or primitive cells of the physical body. In this, the disciple opens the portals of hidden ancestral hates and, in time, he comes to transfer these hostile feelings toward his fellow disciples.

When one has mastered his competitive drives, his soul will quicken his selective palate; he will come to know, intuitively, his nutritional needs.

Science is now opening the door to a better nutrition for mankind. The chemistry of the human body will become once again responsive to the original food commandments given to men.

The ocean bed is a garden of life substances containing nutriment for man. The seeds of the earth are filled with the living substance of the sun—providing longevity. The fruits of the earth, when eaten in their season and in their polarity placements, are exhilarating tonics for the blood.

The desire to store up a reserve in the body comes from a remembrance of famine in this life, or in past lives. The fears which incite men to overeat, or to store up and provide against a scanty period, will be removed; for science is close to perfecting a nutrition for the total peoples of the world. The bodies of men will be lean and symmetrical; and their palates will no longer be subjected to sensuousness.

The Agrarian Angels have been ignored by men who would make synthetic the vital essences within living foods. However, due to the necessity to temper the revolutionary spirit caused by hungry and discontented men, perceptive governments will provide scientists with the means for research in nutrition. Their discoveries will put an end to the destruction of the vital essences in foods. The supply of synthetic food, long imposed on the public, will be replaced by a nutrition harmonious with the body chemistry.

Men in certain parts of the world are surfeited with foods; but they are often over-fed and undernourished. The regime of haste and waste in the affluent parts of the world, and the theme of starvation and fixed tribal food habits in the less affluent parts of the earth now face a 100-year period of nutritional transition. There will enter into the world a nutrition providing man with a diet which will remove him from the aggressive competition as to obtaining food for his body; it will change his competitive aggressions to other levels—the creative, the scientific, and the explorative.

Some persons who are concerned about the "population explosion" are apprehensive that men will be compelled to eat three pills a day and call it nutriment. While this will be necessary in space exploration, it will be untenable for people in the world; for medical and scientific nutritionists will learn that the organs of the body and the digestive system must have bulk nutrition, as well as certain living foods, to sustain the blood. Even as the plant must live upon the atmosphere gathered from the solar energies and the elements, so must the human body depend upon food which contains certain living oxygen gathered from the sun. As long as man has a body with blood, this will be the case.

There were periods in Ann Ree's life when she turned to seafood to supplement her diet, for she found that a living-cell food was necessary to reinforce the ancestral cells in her body. She chose fish because in her spiritual training she had seen that "the fish is a creature without sentient heat, and thus is uncontaminated by the sentient human karma of men." For those who found it necessary to eat meat, Ann Ree recommended lamb, "the only domestic animal insulated from the karmic feelings of men."

In my continued study and association with Ann Ree, much was revealed to me. In the summer of 1952, for a period of several days, I experienced a high fever during which I saw many visions. In one of these visions, I saw a tortoise running at a rapid pace down a road. Ann Ree explained to me that the tortoise is a symbol of the disciple who goes slowly but surely toward his goal. She said, "The tortoise represents yourself, and its rapid pace symbolizes that you have begun to evolve very rapidly of late. One of the reasons for the fever is to slow you down. The title of this vision and lesson is 'The Hasty Tortoise'."

As I became better acquainted with Ann Ree's work, I offered to record and type the telepathic revelations she was receiving at eleven o'clock each evening. Liebschien Muusmann also was present during these sacred moments. Ann Ree began the evening recording period on June 12, 1952 with the following mantram:

There is only One.
There is only one Real.
All of the fears,
Separations, and separateness
Are just illusion.
There is only one Life.
And all Life is seeking God,
And seeking to be Godlike.
There is only one Love.

And all have different degrees of Love.
Love is not to be despised;
It is to be fulfilled
In any or all its parts.
There is one Union in God,
One Peace in mind,
One Love in heart.
We place our minds,
Our hearts,
In Christ,
In Light,
That they may find their home in God.

The evening telepathies from the Masters contained prophetic passages with an initiatory theme. They revealed that Ann Ree had tapped the soul-records of nations; the prototypal relationships in humanities; and the root-ethics within religions. The prophecies were kaleidoscopic in that they touched upon a universal range of subjects. The timing of the prophecies extended from the present age into distant ages. Her evening telepathic experiences between the summer solstice and the autumnal equinox of 1952 provided the manuscripts for three initiatory, revelatory, and prophetic books: *Vision For The Future, The Lively Oracles,* and *Islands of Light.*

In my early years of prophecy, when I worked with persons and their problems, I was subjected to the astral tumults in their lives. My grace protected me; yet something of the astral soil moved into my life—causing unhappiness and discontent with my lot as a prophet. This anguish and discontent remained with me until I discontinued my personal counseling work and reached a higher state of prophecy.

When I came under the tutelage of the Venerable One, I began to understand the mighty workings within the First Heaven. Assisted by the angels, I was able to remain for prolonged periods in the purer atmosphere of Heaven. The holy light and life of the First Heaven were laid open to me. I received the power to research the activities of the Risen Dead, the martyrs, the Saints, the holy men, the sacred Beings, and the Holy Presences—in the First Heaven.

The books, Vision For the Future, The Lively Oracles, *and* Islands of Light, *were recorded during my initiation into the Spheres of Light, or Second Heaven. These Spheres consist of a higher degree of light than the light of the First Heaven. My initiation into the Spheres of Light, or Second Heaven, introduced me to the importance of the cosmic seasons, and opened to me the mystery of the Light-Streams generated by the planetary bodies around the earth. I also learned for the first time that the Rays of the Hierarchy issuing from the constellations around the earth, and the Light-Streams of the planets around the earth, are correlated. I learned that man is initiated emotionally through the astral world; he is initiated through his soul in the First Heaven; he is initiated through his higher mind in the Second Heaven; and he is initiated through his higher self in the Third Heaven, or the Archetypal Realm.*

I learned that the lesser energies of the planetary Light-Streams play upon the lower emotions and lower mentality of man; and that the higher energies of the planetary Light-Streams sustain his spiritual vitality and inspiration. I learned of the great planetary angels overdwelling the planets—the angels who hold the sacred keynote to the planets surrounding the earth.

In the Spheres of Light, or the Second Heaven, I learned through the Masters that all religions given to the world before the time of Jesus had their conception through the astral light; and appealed to the emotions, rather than to the higher minds of men. In their decaying phases, such religions resorted to the ceremonial magics of the astral world. Astral influence was the cause of the deeper sayings of Jesus being deleted or diluted by the early ecclesiastical authorities; for when men know not the difference between the astral light and the spiritual light, they are confused, and their perceptions are faulty.

Over the years Ann Ree had learned through experience to be obedient to spiritual guidance. At Barjona she began to receive telepathic directives and guidance each day at ten in the morning and eleven in the evening. These loving directives were a source of encouragement, comfort and strength, and were the guideposts for the future work.

It became more apparent each day that the work before us would require our full time and attention; therefore we realized that we would have to discontinue our familiar means of earning a livelihood. In a morning telepathic directive from the Venerable One, we were assured that there would be "water plenty and food enough."

Another telepathic directive referred to the years of travel before us as "The Caravan."

Some of the morning and evening telepathic directives were prophetic. Such directives fortified us for the coming days, months, and years. Each time a prophecy was fulfilled we rejoiced—for it proved to us that we were truly walking a destined path.

The telepathic directives were part of each manuscript recording period. The following directives are from the composite telepathy of the Masters, recorded by Ann Ree between June and August 1952.

June 1952

The story of peace is remembered in the heart. Peace is found in strange places. Often it cometh with the face of love; sometimes with the face of work. Peace may come in the lighted face of a friend. But it is always on the note of joy that peace cometh—joy of remembrance of the Father. In peace may be found the steadiness for the cleansing flame. For where purity is and purification cometh, there is peace. There is no friction where purity is.

If thou singest or playest, thou must first have the instrument whole. If thou speakest or writest, thou must speak of the True to be heard. If thou walkest or goest, thou must find a journey for thy feet. And if thou claimest, thou must also prove thyself by the doing, by the being, and by the loving.

Let the starry light fall upon thee as a golden shower of rain. Let each universe reach forth unto thee.

Thy most precious times are when the angelic quiet cometh into thy heart, and when thy mind knoweth what the angel saith unto thy hearing and thy seeing.

Men reach Heaven not by difficult climbings, but men reach Heaven by the simplicity of the giving of the self in love to the One. When one placeth self into the Light, he magnifieth the soul's identity and blendeth with the One.

Men do not by noise or by the making of magical tones reach Heaven; or view Heaven; or receive of Heaven's Light. But men, by love, create the tone by which they travel—the tone by which the angels make possible the passage between earth and Heaven.

Billions of years have set this planet spinning, and thy soul hath accompanied its coming into birth. Thy soul-age is eternal. All that is in thee reflecteth the Divine Universe.

Remember, thou hast taken the strong vow, and there shalt be an encounter with strong works. Count not the cost, or thou shalt be unworthy of the trust. But gather that which is about thee into the singing joy of the going forth in Christ.

Let thy walk be in strength, in dignity, in love, in honor, in peace-staying, in peace-going, in peace-doing. Lose not sight of the angels. Hold fast to the knowledge that thou art not alone.

The work of the beloved keepers of the chalice and servers of the altar now approacheth the time of reaching a rhythm in system—a rhythm in which men shall be trained to share a work-worship. The rhythm of worship shall become as a chalice in the heart. Perfect order and continuity shall follow thee in all of thy works; and each day shall be a diligent day within the Lighted Way.

No door is closed to the seeker, if he intensely desireth and so loveth that he will continue in his search. The path will open to his feet, and he will find entry into that which he seeketh. He hath been promised the Kingdom, but it is through effort that he findeth it and liveth it. It is God's Will that he seek it. It is through God's Love that he findeth the Way and liveth it.

Each day something will be contributed to the work. More and more the over-all plan will be seen. The workshop work will continue until a mass of material is gathered. There will be a downpouring from the direct-archives in Light. This is the beginning of the main portions of the manuscripts.

There will be much rejoicing in the work in February and March.

These are rich days. Reap them and extract their gold and their diamond-dust.

The serious tones of the work overshadow Barjona; but supporting the work is the great joy, the freeing joy—knowing that the work carrieth with it the beam and light toward the New Day, and the call to the heart in light.

The Cherubim Angels work with thee to

keep the equilibrium between thy sense of humor and the seriousness of thy dedication. Humor doth not interfere with the spiritual work. Humor releaseth the tensions and purifieth the stream. It sweeteneth the tone of the spirit.

Let thy love be great, and let thy sharing be done in dignity—and let thy task be taken with simplicity.

The words now being typed are activating a form of telepathy which is entering into the minds of those as yet unknown to thee in the physical world. Telepathic canals are being formed in the minds of eager disciples. Even as the words are being spoken, and then written on the typewriter, they are penetrating the minds of those who are to be ready for the books.

In thy care is the key to open the mysteries of the soul and of Heaven. Thou shalt feel the strength of the opening of the lock. Thou shalt have the answer on the 26th of June in 1953.

Be thou patient; work well, and be strong.

From December until April give all of thy heart; and thou shalt walk for two years in the Jupiter-blue light.* From this the expansion will come, and thou shalt be blessed as a strength-walker of the Way.

Aeons of time and preparation are necessary

---

*We were in California on June 26, 1953. From December 1953 to April 1954 classes were conducted in Los Angeles, Montrose and Burbank, California. In April 1954 we returned to Florida.

to enable the disciple to work in the Hall of Wisdom. The golden grace within the soul chooseth. The need and time place the disciple where he may best work. He first must be qualified in the Inner Worlds. He next is trained and tested in the outer world. The true disciple knoweth that he proveth himself through right works in right timing.

When thou thinkest on work as sacrifice, thou dost not work. But when thou thinkest on work as a craftsman, as a music-maker, as a song-goer, thou hast the joy of the spheres and thou art a sphere-maker.

The student-disciple undergoeth the disciplines, that he may speak the image-language of the Inner Worlds. He accomplisheth this by daily meditation, contemplation, prayer, and mantramic speaking.

When one contemplateth tone and sound, he learneth something of thought waves, and he seeth how thoughts are recorded through vibration. He seeth pure thoughts return to the thinker as harmony; negative thoughts as discord. Each thought of discord hath six destructive wave lengths. One must reach the seventh wave length of thought to think creatively. The disciple learneth to insulate himself from the six lower wave lengths of thought; he maketh a victory over mental discord. He soundeth the seventh wave length of thought, and sendeth his call on the strength of the seventh. When mantrams are spoken, he useth the seventh wave length of tone, sound, and thought—and he createth.*

Thou art being prepared now to serve the twenty-four who will work through the seventy.

Men who spiritually excel in earth have access to the higher thought worlds, where the arrangement of ideas is like a musical keyboard playing upon the human heart. Such spiritual ones become at one with human desire, and work with the pattern of destiny. Pure spiritual thought is a living essence within the Kingdom of God.

July 1952

All over the earth men are beginning to look for Light in what is written, in what is painted, and in what is said. Be on the alert for the Light wherever thou seest it.

From much pain cometh power. From much sorrow cometh seeing.

Each day say to thyself, "I know my way. I know my part." Each day listen to the musics of thy soul, and hear not the call of thy lesser emotions. But hear only the call of the need of the world.

Bring thy design closer to thy vision, and know that others breathe, even as thou breathest, for God.

Remember, thou hast served Him through many lives. And now the day is ready for the

---

*The mantramic formulas were to become catalyst breakthroughs for many who stood close to their thresholds of grace.

healing of the nations. No language separateth thee from a people. No idea separateth thee from universal ideas. No restraint toucheth thee as to journey or flight. Remember, thou hast proved thyself as a philosopher and disciple.

Inspiration is uniquely singled after the pattern of the soul. When a man writeth a book, he writeth from the archives of the karmic past. When he painteth a holy picture, he bringeth forth the vision of Heaven's look. When he painteth his soul's light into a canvas, his soul expandeth; he walketh upon a bridge which man buildeth not with hands—a bridge of light drawing him upward unto God.

This year into 1956 is for the building of a compact plan in which those working will be guided, aided, loved, inspired, and filled with light.*

January 8th beginneth a new and distinct cycle. The geometry within the plan will be placed in its perfect pattern as to the work and workers.

Let those who would be workers become as shepherds; and let them behold always the Star of the Christ in the sky.

August 1952

Many years and many past lives have prepared the building of this work. Reverence and dedication are the results of many lives of spiritual devotion.

*The Niscience Guild of Ethics was firmly established in 1956.

Vary not in thy work. Keep thy counsel. Work quietly, peacefully. That which is organization is that others may be organized. The spreading of the light cometh after the plan hath formulated.

August 17, 1952
Birthday blessing

The voices of the angels speak of a seed planted in the earth. A flower groweth. It is as a sunflower. It turneth into a rosy color. The petals fall and spell the name "TiSeila."

TiSeila standeth within her name, protected from the darts of the earth. She buildeth the golden boundaries. She giveth, and asketh not. She goeth forth with her hand in the Master's hand.

August 31, 1952

Jonathan and TiSeila, thou beginnest thy travels. It is the beginning of a new phase, a new era. Even as the disciples in the days of Jesus were led and guided—words placed in their mouths—so shalt thou be led.

There is rejoicing in the Spiritual Worlds as the Caravan goeth forth. There is rejoicing in the protection. There is also the rejoicing that the things which seek to hold thee back release their hands—and stand and look, while the Caravan moveth into the great vistas of Light.

9
Shadelands

I will instruct thee and teach thee in the way which thou shalt go: I will guide thee with mine eye.

—Psalm 32:8

On July 4, 1952, Ann Ree saw a prophetic vision of the first house on the Caravan. She drew a sketch of the house and said, "We will live in a home in a mountainous region. I feel it to be in the area of the Great Smokies in North Carolina. The house is seated on a high hill, and in the rear is a mountain range. It is a gray two-story dwelling with a long narrow porch. The house slopes down into a winding road. Trees are planted on either side of the walk. It appears to be shady and cool. We will call the house 'Shadelands.' The house will have something to do with dogwood."

When we arrived in Waynesville, North Carolina, on September 2, 1952, a realtor took us to a large ranch house situated high in the Great Smokies. An expansive range of mountains could be seen from the tall windows. We recognized the house to be the one seen in Ann Ree's vision. A road leading to the home was named Dogwood Lane. The house was seated on a partial hill or cliff overlooking a canopy of dogwood trees.

In an environment of indescribable beauty and uninterrupted serenity, the days of the Caravan began. Each moment of the day was seriously and reverently employed. My typewriter began its staccato sound at daybreak. Ann Ree assigned herself the task of bringing in the wood for the large fireplaces, and seeing that each fire was kept burning on the beautiful hearths of this sanctified home. The meals were prepared in a large farmhouse-type kitchen. The dining room, completely surrounded by glass, afforded a panoramic view of the Great Smokies. The changing mood of summer into autumn, the breath-taking sunsets, the joy of being at one with the Heavenly Presences—all contributed to our days of dedication.

In these days Ann Ree became more and more aware that she was receiving from the Higher Worlds information which was desperately needed by earnest disciples. She knew that this information and knowledge must be given to the world at any cost.

Each day we walked in the verdant hills. With my pockets filled with notebooks and pencils, I was ready to write down her observations pertaining to Nature. Many secrets about Nature were disclosed to her on our walks and during the morning recording periods. These recordings provided material for the book *The Venerable One*.

The evening recordings of Ann Ree's telepathic experiences with the Higher Worlds were entirely different from the morning recordings. A major portion of the evening manuscript pertained to the subject of philosophy.

In a morning telepathic directive, the Venerable

One said: "When thou walkest thou art nigh me. When thou makest discoveries, the Master's light revealeth them to thee. In thy walks be alerted to Nature's story, as Nature proportioneth thy mind, thy love. Thou art disciples. Thou livest now in the good ether, in the good light. Peace unto thee."

During one of our walks, Ann Ree was shown by the Venerable One that the root of each tree contains a sacred atom. She learned that "the species of a plant or an animal is determined by the degree of light within the sacred atom. The sacred atom of a tree is in the root, and the sacred atom of an animal is in the genitals. The sacred atom of a man is in the left ventricle of the heart."

While on another walk, I was attracted to a small stone which was half white and half black. Ann Ree explained that this stone was a talisman from the Master—and that the white symbolized the powers of Light, and the black represented the powers of darkness at work in the world.

At Barjona, Jonathan and I had established our rhythms of meditation; however, the days were busy with persons coming and going. In the Great Smokies we were free to devote all of our thoughts to the work. The mountains were sentinels of peace. The dying summer was to me a symbol of my dying to the old and being born to the new. The last vestige of doubt and timidity was removed from my mind and heart; for we were so close to Heaven, and to the beloved Presences who overdirected our labors.

Our manuscripts were precious scrolls received from Heaven, but I knew that the way ahead would not be easy. Though my feet were ready for the road, and my hands held a sacred cargo, I had no illusions; I knew it would be a hard way, a rough way.

At Shadelands I spent many hours of research into the science of the soul. The religious, the mystical, the psychical, the metaphysical, the occult, the esoteric, and the spiritual themes in the world were laid open to me.

I saw the religions of the world and their limitations. I saw that men in the Western world were moving toward a psychological theme in their religions—a theme which would suffocate the mystical side of their faith. I saw the rebellious ones who had removed themselves from formal religions because they felt themselves to be unfed by dogmatic repetition. Such persons resented religions that spoke of Jesus and did not live Him. Many of these persons wandered into metaphysical schools where Jesus was either ignored or considered to be one of the lesser masters; some believed that Jesus was less than Buddha; others thought of Him as just a good man and as other men in earth. Such persons lost touch with their Bible, feeling it to be an allegorical and unrealistic book. These persons moved from one metaphysical group to another. They became omnivorous readers of metaphysical glamour books which temporarily inflated their egos. Their soul-attribute of reverence became dulled. I had met many of this company who believed themselves to be in command of their destinies and who, time after time, defeated the purpose of their souls, forgetting that there were greater laws beyond the circumference of their own desires and wills.

In my ministry I had encountered many untrained, metaphysically-minded persons who thrived upon mental excitation, and who looked for the impossible and the improbable. I had noted that such persons were close to obsession; they were convinced that they could lay down the terms for life—and that God was obedient to them, rather than their being obedient to Him.

I had encountered psychic persons who had crossed the threshold into the lower astral or chimera world. Many of these psychic persons had based their faith upon clairvoyant experience; I saw how they interpreted their visions either in an ecstatic excitation, or in a fearful insinuative manner. Such persons were working with the contraclockwise, rather than the clockwise currents within the solar plexus or psychic brain; thus they saw through a "glass darkly," and the effect was confusion and, often, pandemonium.

It seemed to me that the psychic person was always looking for another psychic to give him the magic word.

Over the years I had seen that the occultist builds his life upon the belief in the negative aspect of karma. His orbit is small. He has possessive associations with friends who are to him fraternity associates bound by a common vow. His occult life is wholly satisfying to him.

The occultist is obedient to certain mental laws. He knows the metaphysical rules; and, when he errs and is corrected, he sees and acknowledges the justice in being reproved. He works for power. While he lacks reverence, he has a deference for his teacher and source of instruction. However, he has a rigidity which prevents him from seeing the necessity for worship.

Should one seek to free himself from the occult coil and give wings to his spirit, his prejudices against all other bodies, religious and metaphysical, are his chief barrier; for his training has been so thorough that he is mechanized to resist all forms of worship.

In my former ministry I had seen that there were many Western persons in the metaphysical way of life who had become strong adherents of Eastern religions. Such persons yearned for a certain peace not found by them in formal Western religions. I saw that the true cause for their compulsion to return to Eastern religious themes was that such persons, in just previous lives, had lived in Eastern bodies; thus they felt more at home with Eastern teachings.

The practice of yoga and of lengthy meditation gave only temporary peace, for the zealous nature of the Western temperament reasserted itself after a period of time. Yoga exercises produced a desire for will-power over others—rather than self-control. Lengthy meditation produced in the Western yoga-disciple a tension within the etheric bodies, creating phantasy and eccentricity.

I saw the esoteric societies in the world to be the philosophical progeny of Schopenhauer, Kant, and Spinoza. I knew that certain esoteric persons had silently imprinted their influence upon many strata of society. However, the secrecy so sacrosanct to the esoteric life would no longer be possible in the scientific age. Such societies, having served their purpose, would disintegrate within this century.

In these revelatory moments I was shown that the light of men's souls is in danger of being obscured by the overwhelming agnostic and materialistic theme in the world. The spiritual life is an enigma to the materialistic mind. The materialistic person relies upon factual proof rather than spiritual cause. When one is dependent upon science alone, this invalidates his faith and short-circuits his intuitive grace regarding God.

I saw that religions had become dangerously complacent, and were in the grips of an insidious inquisition. Atheistic communism on one hand and irreligious psychiatry on the other were two pincer points threatening to crush and demolish the churches of the world.

Religions stood as lambs being led to the slaughter; or like trees being slowly stripped of their bark. The sap of the trees was flowing out of the wounds, and the roots of the trees were in danger of perishing.

I knew that religions had invited these challenges because they had failed to keep alive the holy spirit within the Gospels.

Psychiatry was probing into the shadow-land of man's subconscious mind, ignoring the light of his soul. Psychiatry professed to resolve the discontent and unrest of man by freeing his instinctual passions. Non-religious psychiatry was giving license to amoral actions. The moral ethic, long supported by religion, was in danger of being set aside.

My soul was oppressed with these visions, and I knew there must return to the world a superior theme through religion and worship—a theme touching the soul-hungers of man.

I saw that communism would become socialism; and that psychiatry would in time become cognizant of the soul of man, and of man's need to worship.

My thoughts moved back to the time when I was shown that there are but few truly spiritual persons in the world: one spiritual disciple in every million people. I saw that there are three hundred Good Brothers in the world who work to help men in crisis times; and that there are three thousand dedicated disciples who encircle the globe with their spiritual light. Among these are thirteen telepathic disciples and thirty-three Cosmos Disciples. The thirty-three hundred disciples sustain the Light in the world, and live within the true spiritual ethic as given by the Lord Jesus. As long as these lighted ones live in the world, pure religions will be sustained, and men will find their worship place.

In a vision I saw the world surrounded by a rosy rainbow. I knew this rainbow to be the hearts' blood of men who desired to become at one with God. Though many tongues and creeds separated them, their prayers and their hopes lived through a common need. Men seem to be separate, yet they are integral parts of a whole. I knew that the pressures in the world would open many old wounds. There would be bitterness. And yet, men must let their wounds bleed to make free and pure the life of God within them.

Whatever way stood before me, I prayed for a tongue to speak of God as I knew Him. And I prayed that others would know Him and receive Him.

The following passages are excerpts from the morning and evening telepathic directives recorded by Ann Ree at Shadelands:

September 1952

God moveth the mountains. The Hierarchs carry out the plan of the mountain. The angels work with the elements to aid the Hierarchs.

The Hierarchs' work beginneth its tone as a feather touch. Men feel it not. In the ancient days, when men were martyred for Truth, men believed on martyrdom. In the days of materiality, men believe not. Hierarchy reflections are neither seen nor known by men of opaque temperaments.

The Lord Christ now sendeth His Light onto the mountains and into the deep crypts of the mountain waters. And the virgin country of America, retaining the old of Atlantis, now cometh forth to claim her own.

The Music of the Spheres playeth its work upon the earth. The voice of the angelic tones worketh with the nature spirits. The great Archangels arouse men to their spiritual oneness in God. The Light of the Christ shineth as a great eye into the eye of man—expanding his mind, his vision, his light. Man becometh more creative; more as a creator. He reflecteth upon the image of God. He bringeth forth God's Light into earth; and the dark places of the earth become lighted places. Men find open places in all places.

As the physical world hath governments and laws, so doth the life of the disciple live within the laws of the spiritual realms. He observeth the holiness in all. He feeleth reverence for all.

He seeth beauty and purity in all. Each thing he doeth is through the vision of creation. He leaveth a holy fragrance wherever he walketh.

If the disciple saith, "I live to serve God," he will stand in the overlook and hear the call. And his voice will be lifted unto the sound in God.

He who playeth not becometh a sorry disciple. And he who worketh not becometh a negligent disciple. All blend together that the balance may come.

He who liveth in the higher body of ether, and hath mastered the central pole within the etheric movement, riseth above the slow coil of the earth. The coil then becometh the quickened spiral of the Spiritual Worlds. The slow coil moveth men against one another in oppositions. Men wait in patience. The coil moveth more slowly. That which moveth with the Spiritual Worlds moveth swiftly. He who hath stepped into the grace-stream of discipleship within the Masters' light, love, and telepathy hath stepped into the universals, and he becometh a catalyst in his era or time.

He who walketh in the light of the Masters, and carrieth out his heart action in earth, liveth a life in which each move may be defined as a concentric pattern within a circle. When the mind fulfilleth the spiritual in the Masters' work, the disciple liveth in a circle not defined by men, but which moveth as a central atom or medallion.

He who withdraweth from that which is given to him as physical breaketh the law of the earth. He who maketh his physical life pure through integrity and balance cometh close to the Light. He who chooseth to be eccentric, withdrawn, retreated, withholding in part—is of the mystic, and in danger of becoming the psychic. When the disciple liveth fully, wholly, strongly, carrying the labors of earth, the responsibilities of earth—this bringeth the joyous and the good.

He who standeth outside the gate knoweth not what goeth on in the palace, or the temple. He who standeth outside the palace hateth that which goeth on in the palace. But he who standeth outside the temple crieth to come in. He beginneth the cleansing of his feet that he may climb the stairs. Let thy temple be filled with the welcome light; and let the stairs be as a golden ascent on which all feet may walk.

He who hath been tried in seven lives of martyrdom hath a heart which is loyal. That which is loyalty cometh after many lives of blendings, trustings, and knowings.

Each day as the sun becometh the earth's light in thy sphere of living, thou findest the strength anew to build with love. Thou rememberest that thou didst work in the night hours—and that the spiritual timing between sleep and awakening can be as an eternity for one who carrieth the light in the physical world.

He who starteth the spinning of the wheel,

and rolleth it down a mountain, seeth not always its end in the valley; but he starteth the spinning. Thou startest the wheel; and seest it spinning; and knowest it is well.

Blessings on thee at Shadelands—and to thy work. The mountains which have recorded thy note of joy spread their light and give strength unto thee. Verily shalt those near thee rejoice between the years of 1958 and 1962. And the work thou doest on this mountain top shall find its reward.

Not one thing shall be wasted which toucheth thee in the revealing in Light. The books wait to be born, even as an ego waiteth to come into the earth.

The guidance cometh from day to day. The skills are added each day. The endurance increaseth. And the pattern falleth into its place.

Thy work carrieth itself each day. Thou feelest an increasing steadiness. Thou feelest the sensitiveness which goeth with the going forth unto the Light.

Each day send thy love into the mountain space. The power which cometh to thee in the next twenty-one days cometh not often to many mortals. Let thy soul's power give thee of the good, and strengthen thee for the work.

The Divine Plan is never changed. She who is TiSeila came into the world to finish a work—to finish a work in the Christ-Plan and the Christ-Way. And naught of human, naught of physical, shall change the Plan.

Jonathan is as a reaper—and the harvest is ripe. TiSeila hath planted the grain. She hath seen it grow. She hath been a lonely watcher as the grain grew strong and tall. He who is Jonathan reapeth. He taketh it into a barn; and he bringeth it forth unto man.

October 1952

Blood dropeth from old wounds that are not yet cleansed and healed. When water poureth from a wound, the wound hath its first healing and mending. And when the scar is seen, it is the memory of a lesson. When the scar is white and old, man remembereth—and knoweth in the future what to avoid. When he meeteth the enemy in the forest, he knoweth the poison of his enemy, and he standeth strong.

He who hath had a painful experience need not repeat it again and again; but he retaineth the experience as a lesson, and carrieth it with him as strength for the journey. He carrieth the experience as a reminder—to speak its voice of that which is in himself—of the past weakness. When he recalleth his test and his pain, he remembereth that it was his weakness and not the enemy's weakness that brought him pain.

When the disciple hath found the rhythm of joy which overcometh the astral, he knoweth a pure joy-tone which letteth not melancholy come. The disciple knoweth that when one thread of melancholy cometh between him and the Light, it is as a small hair upon the lens of a camera.

He who is a good disciple, each day discardeth much; and on each day discardeth less; until finally he standeth with God and the Real—having cast aside all of that which is of the unreal. He who cometh with little to discard standeth in the Master's light and love.

Thou shalt have storms. Thou growest strong in storms. Thou shalt not break, though thou bendest. If thou bendest, thou standest.

Remember always the words, "Regardless of the beginnings, thou rejoicest on the endings."

Thou blendest with the star—the star of thy life's quest; the star which saith always to the children in light, "Thou art sons in light, and thou art of the Father's Love. Thou knowest no will save His Will. And thou knowest no light save the Light which cometh from Him."

That which cometh as the tongues of the serpents—which would try to destroy the work—is of the dark. Thou now findest the power to overcome that which standeth between thee and the Light.

Thou hast the courage which cometh from not knowing when thou art defeated. And thou goest on beyond the point of defeat into victory.

Thou walkest now abreast with Nature. Thou takest in each day the odors, the fragrance, the life. Thou buildest them into the mind and into the glands.

In the light, each day, Nature healeth thee. Thou couldst not have worked in any other way. Thou couldst not have continued on in any other way.

Thou walkest now in the Master's bowknot, protected in love and light.

That of the West now standeth as a beckoning hand. And the West maketh it possible for thee to bring the Jupiter light. But what thou bringest thou wilt perfect before thou touchest the West.

Thou, Jonathan, in the night hours of thy sleep, didst see and witness the working of the dark. Thou didst see that the dark are those who work with cunning minds. Thy lesson was to see that the cunning mind standeth between the disciple and his battle for Light—and that he who is of the dark and the force in the world worketh now to kill and crush out the love in earth. He who hath the Light in him shineth forth, and he loveth. Even though it killeth him by the sword, he loveth; and he letteth not the dark in. And in all things he loveth, and worketh, and serveth.*

Thou now facest the time when thou beginnest thy first step; the balance across the rope over the chasm. Thou holdest a rod, balancing as thou walkest. Thou lookest not below, but ahead to the goal on which the light of the

---

*This directive is the interpretation of the following dream: I first saw the words "Genghis Khan." Then there were several soldiers in uniform who were kneeling in front of an altar in a holy building. If one of the soldiers were seen to have the slightest trace of reverence, a man with a bow and arrow would shoot him in the heart.

sacred mountain awaiteth thee. Thou hast walked the rope before. Thou knowest it with familiar feet. Thou losest not thy balance.

Jonathan, thou didst ask why a special acorn becometh a mighty oak, and why other acorns fall to the earth and die. The acorn that becometh a tree hath been selected by the angels because it containeth the atom-germ for a tree. So is a disciple selected because he hath quickened the spiritual atom which openeth his mind and heart to Heaven.

The Lords of Karma sift out the weak, and the Lords of Individuality sustain the spiritually strong in the world. The Lords of Karma give respite to those who fall by the wayside, so that the weak may work to become strong in another day. The Lords of Individuality sustain the strong ones who stand forth in the trials.

TiSeila, often when thou awakenest in the morn, the load on thy shoulders seemeth heavy on one side and light on the other side; but when thou walkest in the Light, thou hast seen by nightfall that the load is the same on both shoulders.

10

The Archetypes

For this God is our God for ever and ever: he will be our guide even unto death.

—Psalm 48:14

After seven fruitful weeks in the mountain fastness of the Great Smokies, we were guided to move from North Carolina to New York City. Before leaving Shadelands, Ann Ree predicted that we would see the Hudson River from our new living quarters.

We arrived in New York City on a cold, windy day in October 1952. Unable to find suitable apartments facing the Hudson River, we moved into an apartment building that appeared to have no view of the river. We wondered about the prophecy—until we found a small side window from which we could see a minute portion of the river. Thus the prophecy was fulfilled, but in a manner unforeseen by our human interpretation or expectation. This was my first insight into the level of prophetic guidance which manifests unique conclusions. Sometimes, such guidance has a humorous ending; always, it contains a lesson in faith.

The Higher Worlds gave a name to each significant point on the Caravan where we received important manuscript. This assured us that our temporary environments were blessed. The names proved to be a comfort to us as we moved from place to place. Some of the names were Wooded Place, Circle-in-the-Sun, Cherubim House, Still Waters; and, after Shadelands, our New York living quarters—Shelter.

Thomas Sugrue was living in New York City at this time—and Ann Ree was looking forward to discussing with him the telepathic manuscript. However, each time she tried to call him, she was diverted; a wall of "frozen ether" fell between them. A short time later she learned of Thomas Sugrue's death. She then knew that the reason she had not been able to contact him was due to a heavenly intervention which surrounds the dying, giving the one dying privacy in the hours of his release from life.

Ann Ree saw in a vision the man who would publish her first completed manuscript. She described his appearance, even the features of his face, and said that he would be suffering from a loss of some kind. Eight months later, when we walked into the office of the DeVorss Publishing Company in Los Angeles, California, we both recognized Mr. DeVorss as the man seen in her vision, and we learned that a few days earlier he had lost his wife in childbirth.

Wherever we traveled on the Caravan, we observed the Sunday morning worship rhythm. Each worship service was blessed by the Great Immortals and the Angel of the Presence.

Worship rhythms are first activated in the Spiritual Worlds. To ignore these rhythms is to place one's self out of timing in his physical and spiritual affairs.

While conducting our Sunday worship service in

New York City on December 7, 1952, Ann Ree made the following prophecy:

> Holy magnetism will be recovered in the worships of men. Men will worship in small places, in dwelling places, and in homes. The true spiritual dramas will be carried on in small buildings made shrinelike by the hands of those who dedicate their lives. The small sanctuaries will become alive with the early Christian mystical power of love.
>
> Large churches will become social institutions for the lesser cultures in religion—and training will be given in religious history. In the larger churches the moral ethic will be revived. Great pomp, glamour and ceremonies will be modified and changed.
>
> Worship within the small sanctuary will include the silence of meditation in which sincere, dedicated disciples will build a ring-pass-not through their devotion and love. Their prayers, meditation, and devotions will contribute to world healing; and their worship will enable those who have lost their way to enter the portals of their souls. The Angel of the Presence and the Cherubim Angels will provide an unseen ritual which will be equally distributed among those who have dedicated and pure hearts.

The Masters called Ann Ree "a stubborn receiver" because it was her policy to prove any telepathy she received. She was told that the Higher Worlds considered stubborn receivers to be valiant disciples, for such disciples refused to be victims of lower or insidious astral telepathies. In her initiations Ann Ree learned to identify seven levels of telepathy:

1. Man-to-man telepathy
2. Ancestral telepathy
3. (a) Atavistic telepathy from past lives
   (b) Telepathy from the egotistical acts of former lives
   (c) Telepathy from the earthbound dead
   (d) Insidious astral telepathy
4. (a) Angel and Cherubim telepathy
   (b) Telepathy from the Risen Dead
5. (a) The soul level of telepathy
   (b) Memory of grace lives
   (c) Memory of talents and achievements of good in past lives
   (d) Telepathy from the higher self
6. Mediative telepathy from a fellow disciple
7. Telepathy from the Higher Worlds and Holy Presences of Heaven.

The evening manuscript recordings often contained telepathic passages from one named "Fleur de Lis"—the symbolic name of a highly evolved disciple living on the European continent. We learned that Fleur de Lis is a scientist in the physical world, and a Cosmos Disciple in the Higher Worlds. His spiritual work is unknown to his contemporaries and associates in the world.

Ann Ree's telepathic association with the Masters had made her familiar with the method of transposition in light with the various Light-Streams of the Masters. Due to her long training in the Masters' light, she had come to know through countless instances the flawless purity in this association. While writing *Islands of Light,* she learned that Fleur de Lis also was working in the Masters' light and that he had full awareness of the intermediary processes within the Higher Worlds. In New York Ann Ree began to receive daily communication from Fleur de Lis through spiritual mediative telepathy. Fleur de Lis' training in science and astronomy, and his dedication as a Cosmos Disciple, enabled him to extend Ann Ree's understanding of the new spiritual philosophy being born in the scientific age.

One evening I painted a small portrait of a famous man in history. The painting went smoothly and was accompanied by a feeling of joy. When I completed the painting, Ann Ree saw that the personage I had painted was a former life of Fleur de Lis. After gaining knowledge of his past life, she entered more freely into their daily telepathic communication.

The telepathy Ann Ree received from Fleur de Lis differed from the telepathy she received from the Masters. The telepathy from Fleur de Lis was more scientific and factual, while the telepathic manuscript from the Masters contained more parables and allegories.

Because of the time difference in the continents, Fleur de Lis often used the "banked recording" technique of telepathy—that is, his telepathic thoughts and ideas first remained quiescent in the sensitive telepathic zones of Ann Ree's brain. The Recording Angels preserved the ideas within the banked recordings, and, when the time and event were ripe, the scientific ideas were released into her stream of consciousness.

Ann Ree was very careful to observe the ethic pertaining to a ready circuit from mind to mind. Thus, she never turned to Fleur de Lis for the answers to her personal concerns. These two disciples were able to work together because of their former lives of catalyst association.

When disciples are catalysts to each other, their heart atoms and their mental atoms are in alignment, and the telepathy between their minds becomes "a coherent stream." The coherent stream of telepathy is impersonal, and pertains to the eternal verities or truths residing within the archives of Heaven.

Jesus said, "For where two or three are gathered together in my name, there am I in the midst of them" (St. Matthew 18:20). This is a demonstrable truth. When two disciples rise above the conflicts of duality and devote themselves to serving the Real, they become mediators between earth and Heaven.

Catalyst association is the result of an unwavering trust between disciples—a trust built over many harmonious lives together, in which some significant purpose was shared and fulfilled.

The disciple is not always aware of the source of his ideas. However, as he becomes more spiritually sensitive, he sees that there are rhythmic cycles within creative thinking, and that there are many sources of telepathic mediation. He realizes that he is not the sole possessor of the creative fiat, and that there are many laborers in the vineyard of creation in Heaven and in earth.

The disciple dedicated to the Christ strives to purify himself and his thoughts—and, in time, the light of his soul enables him to define the various levels of telepathic, creative thought.

The evening telepathic manuscript in New York City revealed the name of another Cosmos Disciple—the Hollander. Even as Fleur de Lis used a symbolic name, so did the Hollander use a "blind" rather than his true name. The Hollander is a religious leader living in Europe. His invisible activities as a Cosmos Disciple are known only to those who work with him telepathically.

We first learned of the Hollander in November 1952 when he tried to establish telepathic rapport with Ann Ree through the Masters' light. She found it difficult to align her thoughts with his telepathy—and after several attempts the Hollander discontinued his telepathic sending. Five months later, during Easter 1953, the Hollander finally established perfect alignment with Ann Ree. Their telepathic association resulted in her recording an illuminative manuscript about the life of Jesus. The Hollander was qualified to transmit this manuscript about Jesus, even as Fleur de Lis, a scientist, was qualified to present knowledge about the eternal atoms.

Ann Ree wondered why she was the one chosen to bring forth these important manuscripts. She was told that the great spiritual renaissance would take place in the Western Hemisphere, and that her placement, grace, and qualifications as a telepathic disciple with logos made her the suitable one to give birth to the manuscripts.

Fleur de Lis and the Hollander know each other in the physical world, but their work as telepathic mediators for the Higher Worlds is known only to a few. They are two of the thirty-three Cosmos Disciples who are scattered throughout the earth. The thirty-three Cosmos Disciples are known as the Sacred 33.

There are thirteen telepathic disciples in the world. They are the outer-world representatives of the thirty-three Cosmos Disciples. When a Cosmos Disciple's life is concluded, a telepathic disciple becomes a Cosmos Disciple, and an advanced disciple becomes a telepathic disciple. In this manner there is a continuous stream of spiritual ideas flowing into the world.

The Masters will no longer re-embody in the physical world. The thirty-three Cosmos Disciples have inherited the mantles of the Masters.

The Cosmos Disciples work in the various polarities of the earth. These Disciples are the mediative balance wheels in the vocations contributing to the human spirit. Cosmos Disciples may be found in varied fields of action: science, art, music, religion, education, finance, statesmanship, medicine, engineering, anthropology, archeology, nutrition, chemistry, physics, geophysics, astronomy, space science, biology, entomology, zoology, oceanography, agriculture, architecture, and in other areas of human endeavor.

The thirty-three Cosmos Disciples are great telepathic reservoirs of Inner-World receiving, memory, and transubstantiation. In this, they become, as Fleur de Lis and the Hollander, the senders onto those who are in alignment with them in discipleship.

In December 1952, Ann Ree completed the second eighty-day rhythm of evening manuscript. On the night she began a new telepathic series, something unusual occurred: instead of immediately recording her visions and inner hearing, she remained silent for several minutes before speaking. When she finished recording, we looked at each other with expressions of surprise, for the manuscript was unlike any received previously. Explaining why she did not speak during the first minutes, she said, "I could find no human words to describe what I was experiencing and seeing!"

Ann Ree had moved into a new level of telepathic revelation, and had begun to research a higher Heaven than the Second Heaven. She had crossed the "vibrancy barrier" between the Second Heaven and the Third Heaven. In the Third Heaven dwell the original archetypes of God; these archetypes are the blueprints for the creation of the earth.

The first telepathic directive accompanying the new manuscript contained these words: "Even as the thread on the recorder moveth, so doth the thread move between TiSeila and the Spiritual Worlds. This thread moveth through her eternal atoms, and she is shown the description of creation. In the archetypal kingdom she will meet a wider rhythm, which demandeth more of her inner hearing and seeing in the Light."

On the following evenings Ann Ree recorded in pure logos what she saw and heard while viewing the archetypes. At first, her research in the Third Heaven was made possible by the mediative assistance of Fleur de Lis and ten other Cosmos Disciples. The atoms in her higher etheric body were fortified by the eternal atoms of Fleur de Lis and the eternal atoms of the ten other Cosmos Disciples. The combined atom body of light of these Cosmos Disciples enabled her to begin her alignment with the Archangels, so that she could behold and interpret the archetypes.

When Ann Ree used her prophetic powers to give aid to persons in distress, she worked with the Guardian Angels of the persons in need. In the Spheres of Light (Second Heaven), where she received the prophetic books, she worked with the Recording Angels of the world and with the Masters. When Ann Ree received the power to interpret the archetypes, she became a prophet for the Archangels—and her prophecies were revelatory rather than clairvoyant.

The prophetic power stemming from communion with the Archangels pertains to the creation of the world and its fulfillment. Such prophecy speaks of the universal whole, and becomes a voice for the Christ—telling of His work, and of its effect upon the earth and upon other earth systems.

When Ann Ree used the power of clairvoyant prophecy, her vision was single. When she communed with the Saints and the Risen Dead, her vision was two-fold: inner seeing and inner hearing. When she received from the Masters in the Spheres of Light, her vision was three-fold: her inner eye, inner ear, and speech became as one instrument of illumination. She reached this state of three-fold vision when she dictated the three prophetic books, *Vision for the Future, The Lively Oracles,* and *Islands of Light*. When she became a telepathic revelator for the Archangels, her vision became four-fold, and she entered into a fourth dimensional consciousness. Assisted by the Archangels—the great Guardians of the archetypes—she began to receive directly from the archetypes. In the four-fold vision, she saw through the light of the archetypes; the greater archetones [or the Word] were opened to her ears; she heard the creative hum of the universe; her own logos became at one with the Holy Ghost; and her mind received *knowing* in the Light of the Christ.

In her first research of the archetypes, Ann Ree saw how the earth was created. To better prepare herself for the new, deeper, and more exacting work, she began to make pastel pictures of the visions she was seeing of the creation of the sun, the earth, and the planets. After concluding this series of paintings, she had no difficulty in sustaining her alignment with the Archangels protecting the archetypes.

New York has always held a pathos for me. This city has moved me and inspired me. My individuality was enveloped by mass thoughts and feelings; my wonder consciousness and moods were keen, alert. In this city of New York I gave birth to a child; I grew to be a woman; I placed my heart and my trust in the Master.

When I observed once again the tall skyscraper canyons against the skyline of New York City, I realized that I had concluded a twenty-eight year cycle. It was here in this vast city I first spoke to the Master, saw his face, and began my serious quest for the Light. The quiet mediative hours under the Master's instruction in the first naive days of my spiritual training were still fresh in my mind. And now once again, as in those first days, I was painting the story of the creation of the earth. (Twenty-eight years earlier I had painted the kabalistic story of creation.) The windows of my soul were at last open. The atoms of my mind sang with the cosmos nuances of creation. All of the days, months and years of my reaching, praying, and teaching were at last to yield up their fruits.

When I finally coordinated my inner ear with the hum of the archetones within the greater archetypes, I experienced a tumbling cascade of telepathic communication. There were no tensions accompanying the visions and revelations. Everything I saw and heard had a revelatory theme. There were periods when the crescendo of spiritual power was so great that I was caught up into an ecstasy of extreme holiness and joy. In the daytime hours I would often be filled with a feeling of insufficiency, for I saw that an overwhelming responsibility had been placed in my hands. I was frightened and humbled. I wondered how I could translate and communicate to the minds of others the glorious spectacles of the Third Heaven.

Words I had never encountered in my former experience were heard and added to my vocabulary. Terminology which was so apt was given to me to describe the procedures in creation. By degrees, this new vocabulary became my own. It now remained for me to transpose to others the knowledge I had received.

When I touched the Realm of Light, or the Third Heaven, the plan in cosmos was opened to me. I learned of the greater archetypes, and of the universal rhythmic compulsions—and I saw universal vistas and dramas.

I was shown that there are three archetypal actions affecting the earth: (1) the greater archetypes, (2) the moving archetypes, and (3) the destroying or sealed-in archetypes. When the three archetypal systems coincide in their actions, men in the world experience emotional, mental, and religious chaos. The outer friction caused by this combined spiritual fire purifies the masses, and prepares for a new era in which men will aspire once more to come nigh to their souls.

The greater archetypes *in the Third Heaven, or Realm of Light, are throbbing, humming vortices of intelligence. These archetypes are the connecting link between the outer universe and the universe of man. The greater archetypes are opened to holy seers only when men on earth are prepared to receive eternal and spiritual ideas.*

The Archangels, working with the Christ, preside over the greater archetypes. The Christ Spirit is the Archetypal Presence permeating the greater archetypes. When the telepathic disciple unites himself with a composite telepathy in the Third Heaven, he is taught directly by what he sees and hears in the greater archetypes.

He who rises to the world of the greater archetypes communes with the Archangels overdwelling and protecting the archetypes. Through the help of the Archangels, he sees the eternal and eternity blueprints, and he records them upon his mind.

The greater archetypes work with the Will of God. *The Archangels sustain and maintain the rhythms of the archetypes. When men are ready to receive the greater ideas of Light, the Holy Ghost releases the tones or archetones within the archetypes—and saviours, holy seers and prophets transpose and reveal the ideas of Light to men.*

The greater archetypes form a cohesive body, enabling the Christ to center His Light in this earth system. The world is now undergoing a cleansing, so that men may prepare to receive the archetypal Light of the Christ. Institutions, barriers, and broken idols will be replaced by the true fire of the living God—through which the Christ, the Regent of the earth, makes His Presence known to men.

When men are reluctant to believe in God, the world falls into a tumultuous chaos. During a chaos period, a nucleus of advanced disciples is born to the earth. These disciples know one another in the Spiritual Worlds. They have made a covenant and a vow, and they are protected from the forces of the dark. Their work is to bring the Word of the Kingdom of God; and from their teachings the hearts of men are made more humble.

The moving archetypes *dwelling within the Second Heaven are three-dimensional reflections of the greater archetypes. These archetypes work with the* laws of God. *The moving archetypes move upon men every ten thousand years, and stir them to form new religions; to transform racial impulses; to build societies; to support the moral ethic protecting families, communities, and religions; and to produce ingenious inventions suitable to the era or the age.*

The destroying *or* sealed-in archetypes *reside in the core of the earth. These archetypes are absorbed by men into their emotions when men become decadent, agnostic, corrupt. The destroying archetypes tear down old systems and formulas, so that the greater archetypes may touch the minds and souls of men in the world.*

The destroying or sealed-in archetypes are reflected in the lesser regions of the astral world. When men see these archetypes, they "know in part"; they come under the fear of the wrath of God; their prophecies and their dreams are colored by subtle fears.

When men come under curses, they are under the influence of the destroying or sealed-in archetypes. Only their Guardian Angels may free them from the devitalizing conditions invoked through harmful or cursing thoughts.

Before mankind as a whole can receive the spiritual impulses sent forth from the greater archetypes, certain egos are born to the world—egos whose purpose is to work as ambassadors for the destroying or sealed-in archetypes. Having lived many negative lives, they become karmic pawns in society. Their negative, destroying tendencies make them ideal tyrants for destruction. When old systems are to be erased, rulers with agnostic hearts feel compelled to overthrow governments, societies, and religions.

When glacial periods and earth cataclysms—such as earthquakes, floods, volcanic eruptions, and tidal waves—occur, the sealed-in or destroying archetypes are at work. During these times men die, that they may be reborn in periods more suitable for their evolvement. Those who survive are shepherded or herded into continents waiting to know the hand and skills of man.

In June 1952, while in Florida, Ann Ree recorded a telepathic directive containing these words, "When Venus is in Pisces, the Master will make himself known to Jonathan."

Venus remained in Pisces during the latter part of our stay in New York City. I was satisfied that the prophecy had been fulfilled, for the daily manuscripts and directives were ample proof to me of the Master's presence. On the evening that Venus was to leave Pisces, Ann Ree and I were working quietly on pastel drawings. Suddenly, I saw a flash of light streak across the floor of the room. Ann Ree saw a great ball of light, and heard it explode with a tremendous sound. She then saw Master R. He told her that the light we had seen was the releasing of a spiritual atom containing the archetype or blueprint for our new work.

After I had familiarized myself with the archetypal record of creation and had seen the virginal archetypes of unborn nations and continents, I next studied the archetypes for the humanities of the earth and saw how men were imaged in twelve prototypal forms. I was then shown the archetypes of the animal kingdom and the archetypes of the plant kingdom. When this research concluded, I was permanently united with an archetype called the Niscience* Archetype. *I was told that the hum of this Archetype is now sounding to the world, and will bring a new spiritual impulse. The world was unprepared to receive the Niscience Archetype before the scientific age. The Niscience Archetype will unite men with the Jesus*

---

* Pronounced NISHence

Ethic, and will bring them closer to the Christ—thus producing in the scientific age a new theme of devotion and dedication.

The following passages are excerpts from the diary of telepathic directives recorded by Ann Ree in New York City:

November 1952

When thou placest thy works in the hands of the ready, remember those who receive them shall have had their vision opened through the stigmata of pain.

Those who aid thy work in the next five-year pattern make eternal grace for themselves. Those who have the courage to aid make greatness for their future.

Thy soul-light belongeth to thy soul. Thy soul belongeth to thy higher self. Thy higher self belongeth to God. When thou listenest to the higher self, thou shalt hear the answers recorded within thy soul's tone; and thou shalt hear the rejoicing of the angels in the Spiritual Worlds.

December 1952

Let the winged bird light thy way. Let the flight be not fearful. Let the Invisible Sun light thy pathway. Let the luminous cloud of thy soul's light reflect the great Light and World of God. Let the reason within thy consciousness-mind reflect thy soul-tone's harp.

Thou who walkest among the archetypes, fear not; for thou hast found the path unto the Ways and Light of God. And thou now relatest thyself to the path of the whole in God. Cleanse thy heart and let thy will be laid aside, and stand in the Will of God.

Thou art standing in the shadow of the Almighty when thou dost stand in the great archetypes. Thou art standing in the Great Silence, where dwelleth the great soundless Word. The soundless sound placeth its hum upon thy throat; and from thy throat cometh the words to express it.

He who dedicateth himself to logos and the great archetypes hath found his freedom in the Invisible Worlds.

He who goeth into the great archetypal realm goeth with his body of light. His higher etheric body is the instrument of his moving, and the atom between his brows becometh co-atom to the central atom of the Christ. He traveleth over the astral world, touching only the higher regions of the astral planes; he moveth through the world of tone, through the Spheres of Light, and onto the Realm of Light. Here, he is given the vision of the workings within the archetypal realm. He is accompanied by disciples who have lived many dedicated lives as disciples. He beginneth his work in Light, that he may aid the great Hierarch Beings and the Christ.

The etheric garment used by the disciple in the Spheres of Light becometh a garment of akasic flame or fire, that he may function in the Realm of Light. This garment is a garment of luminosity, sending forth great rays of spiritual light. He liveth within the exalted Breath of God. He beginneth to have access to the sacred miracles. This enableth him to help men accelerate their timing and receive their grace.

Disciples in light become creators in the sending of great pictorial ideas, which become the future creative thoughts of men. All disciples in light are aided by the great Masters, by the Great Teacher, or the Lord of Lords.

The former unfathomable things of God are to be given with simplicity; they will intrude not upon men's consciousness, nor violate the mental world or the physical actions of men. The Great Teacher now moveth His Light closer to the earth, for men are ready to receive and understand the greater mysteries of cosmos and God.

The psychic nature of man is now being muted, and pure telepathy between mind and mind will be understood. The telepathic work from mind to mind will increase in the disciples in light. Those living in the physical world, who work with the invisible body of the Christ, will send their great showerings of light, their symbologies, and their sacred-vowel alphabets (mantrams) through spiritual light. These will resound to mankind, and prepare men for the changing currents in the world.

All disciples are placed in environments unique to their capacities and their expressions.

Wherever Light is needed, the disciple is sent. His soul's impulse will give him his direction.

Man standeth and vieweth his beginnings—the vaulted heavens, the fiery space. He standeth encentered in God's World. When man hath acquired the vehicles, the mind, the light, and the love to penetrate these portals, he will make his entry into these great vistas.

When man traveleth on a journey in the earth, he maketh his passage either by labor or effort; or he earneth his passage and applieth himself to his journey. So it is with the journey into the Father's home and into the Spirit's beginning.

When man hath acquired the means by which he maketh the passage, he will make the journey into the Spheres of Light and recover the tones ringing true to his soul-tone. The disciple in light maketh his passage into the Realm of Light when he hath opened his eternal and spiritual atoms.

He who studieth the stars seeth them in the midnight blackness, silver and bright against the great canopy of the sky. He thinketh not of them as brothers and sisters, but he thinketh of them as cold faces shining and distant. When he cometh to understand the breadth of God, the length of God, the height of God, the depth of God, he shall truly know each starry face is a mirror revealing the light of his soul from other days—when he dwelt in other stars before he made the pilgrimage onto this earth. He shall see God not as a God of vengeance, but he shall see the earth as a mighty and glorious place in which men each day prove the Law and Love of God.

The light in the spiritual atoms of the thirteen telepathic disciples makes atom points throughout the world. The ideas received by the telepathic disciples, and things seen within the great archetypal worlds, are recorded within a ventricle of the brain heretofore not used by man. This ventricle for the receiving of telepathy will become more sensitive in the scientific age. The telepathic disciple hath opened a lighted passage in the skull which enableth him to record and to remember the instruction he receiveth from the archetypal worlds.

He who hath logos will speak of the archetypal ideas and write of them. He who is scientific will bring them as mercy-inventions to the world. He who hath art will bring them as creation. He who hath music will bring them as masterful composition.

It is the telepathic disciple's work to build the body of luminosity, and to recall the archetypes in their order; and to transpose them to men as ideas—that men may begin a new form of creation.

The steel in the disciple is tempered. The gold is cast into a mighty furnace. The pearl is brought forth from its hidden place. The emerald is extracted from the healer's crucible.

The amethyst cometh forth and maketh a stylus with which to engrave the tablets. The ruby shineth forth even as the red blood of man. All of these give the disciple the coloring of his own atoms' light—building the body of luminosity.

That which is reverence buildeth the body for the Light. That which is the exact mind buildeth the plan for the Light. That which is courage buildeth the spiritual fire.

The earth is a planet for consciousness. The earth is the planet of man's progression. It is the planet of discipleship. It is the planet in which man transformeth matter into Spirit. It is the planet in which man giveth his mind to the Christ, his body to the Hierarchs' work, and his spirit to God. It is the planet which man will make into a star through the light within his consciousness.

All planets surrounding the sun assist the earth in her destiny. The planets establish an equilibrium for men on earth—spiritualizing men with the Holy Fire of the Christ.

Man receiveth insight into God through many lives of intuition, experiment, experiencing, suffering, the gathering of knowledge, and the obtaining of wisdom.

In the process of the progressions to come in the future years, men shall name the archetypes by many names, and shall acknowledge their existence by many conditions. But men shall not call them the divine archetypes. The scientific world shall give a name to the archetypal system, for science shall recognize that there is an Intelligible Will bringing all things to perfection by degrees.

Within the next three hundred years, Greater Cosmos will possess men, even as lesser cosmos has possessed them until now. When men come under the influence of Greater-Cosmos ideas for an extended period of time, a new age beginneth in the world, and the souls of men respond to the Light of God.

There are periods in which the greater archetypes are more active than in others, and more effulgent with the Word. When the world is ripe or ready to receive the greater ideas from the Third Heaven, the Holy Ghost speaketh through the exalted tones or higher archetones within the greater archetypes. When the greater archetypes are dormant, men must depend upon the moving archetypes for their religious and moral impulses.

Christmas Day 1952

On this Christ morn, receive thy mantle of illumination from the Christ. Keep holy thy vows of dedication, so that thou wilt be prepared for the greater things coming to thee. Let this day be as a mighty pause of peace. Thou bringest thy treasures to the Christ. He giveth thee a blessing on this morn.

Let him who writeth with a prophet's pen write with a pure heart, and let him see with a reverent eye.

January 1953

The Archangels working with the archetones keep man's faith alive. The Archangels use the great tones in the Third Heaven to sustain man's belief in God. The Archangels working with other angels keep certain layers of the heart, mind, and soul awake to the spiritual verities of Heaven. Were it not for the Archangel-tides, men would fall into desolateness.

The Archangels cannot reach men who turn their beliefs toward physical exaltedness rather than spiritual exaltedness.

The covenant of the Archangels is to work with God, the Father, the Hierarchs, the Christ, and the Holy Ghost. The Archangels are the custodians of the tones within the greater archetypes.*

The Archangels go before all men in new beginnings. They assist in the birth and death of planets; in the birth and death of all seed life. They assist in the birth and death of man. The Archangels work with the birth and death of races and nations. They aid the Angels of Birth and Propagation. The Archangels work with

---

*The Host of Archangels working with the archetypes send forth the Archangels Raphael, Gabriel, Michael, and Uriel during the four cosmic seasons of the year, so that men will open their souls and their minds to the uplifting impulses of Heaven. Raphael works with the vernal equinox; Uriel, the summer solstice; Michael, the autumnal equinox; Gabriel, the winter solstice.

all things which have a seed in earth. They work with the human seed to be born; and they work on the sacred-atom seed of the heart which enableth man to die.

The Archangels of Saturn aid men to cross the vista of death—and death becometh a peaceful sleep and repose. He who dieth receiveth his recordings through his personal Guardian Angel, his Recording Angel, and through the Lords of Karma; and receiveth his peace through the great love of the Archangel power.

The telepathic disciple liveth always in the knowledge of other disciples and their work in earth. He liveth in the knowledge that he is accompanied by other disciples throughout the earth. And he liveth in the knowledge that separateness between disciples is one of the greatest sins; and that he who separateth himself breaketh the link between disciples. He knoweth that the blending in discipleship is as necessary as air to breathe. He who hath the power of discipleship and cutteth the cable between himself and another disciple hath affected all disciples. The disciple liveth and breatheth and moveth in light, that he may keep forever the tone of blending with all disciples.

All disciples have lived in many eras and times so that their spiritual atoms might become antennas of sensitivity. Through many lives of countless sacrifices, expressions, and evolvements—and always through the love of labor and light—the disciple produceth the combining-atoms which unite him with his fellow disciples and the Presences of Heaven.

The disciple increaseth his stature from life to life. Through creative embodiments he increaseth the light within his body of light.

The telepathic disciple looketh back and seeth that he hath been the lesser disciple, the lay disciple, the evangelistic disciple, the patriarch disciple, the prophetic disciple, the disciple of light. And he seeth that in time he will become the Cosmos Disciple.

The telepathic disciple standeth in simplicities, but also in grandeur. The earth becometh as a small globe in the palm of his hand; he discerneth the greater archetypes. He relateth himself to the earth with pity and uttermost tenderness. And he seeth all of its convolutions and its evolvings, and all of the great spiritual participants working with the earth. He seeth mighty and wondrous things unfolded and revealed through the light of telepathy. And he knoweth that the minds of men swim as in a Saturn sleep, covered by a sulphurous, foglike cloud over the mental body. The disciple seeth that the cloud now beginneth its dispersing, and that light cometh swiftly onto man.

He who liveth within the mental cloud will receive the light as a lightning blast; and he will begin to see other degrees of light rather than his own egotistical light.

It is through the angelic stream that the

luminosity body of the telepathic disciple is enabled to rise. Through the angelic accompanying, he is enabled to look on the Archangels' work with the planets and with the fiery core of the earth. He beholdeth the working of the Race Angels. He seeth how nations and races evolve through karmic timings. These things are shown to the disciple through the angels and the Archangels.

Night-flight for the telepathic disciple becometh a matter of organized ether and organized light. The design which he carrieth out in the day cometh from the plans made with his higher self in the night. Through grace he hath earned the right to rise into the higher Spheres and Realms of Light.

Karma and entanglement remain not long in the life of the telepathic disciple. The telepathic disciple riseth above the entanglements and disengageth himself—that he may work in the right harmony and the right environment.

There are no exceptions in karma for the telepathic disciple. He payeth his karmic debts with the unique dividends of grace; and he findeth strength to disengage himself from that which restraineth him.

When men come to the time in which they will relate themselves to the greater archetypes, the moving archetypes, and the sealed-in archetypes, they will have perfected the greatest system in mathematics; their understanding will be through the four-fold consciousness; they will have penetrated space; and they will have mastered relativity and time. They then will have come to the point of the spiritual equation working within the Christ, the Father, and God.

Not one thing is unrelated to the plan in cosmos. The karmic laws seem to produce deformities and maladjustments, but these laws bring into balance that which hath been sown in many lives of other days. If men had not created and accumulated karma or debts through the laws of sowing and reaping, the laws of retribution, the laws of consequence, or the laws of cause and effect, they could not have used the weighing and analyzing facet of their thoughts; nor would they have the power to create.

Even as the silkworm createth that which maketh the silk and its preciousness in garment, so doth man, through the alternating currents of karma, create within himself and of himself. Man's work on earth is to create, and to become as the Jesus man.

When men begin to realize the simplicity within the plan of Greater Cosmos, when science unrolleth her great secrets, and when each thing showeth its relating as of the physical to the spiritual and the spiritual to the physical, the World of God will be a part of man's life, even as breathing—even as the earth, the air, the fire, and the water about him. He will take for granted the spiritual things in the World of God as he taketh for granted the natural things in the world of the earth. But until man learneth of these correlatings through his own direct experience, he will relate himself to the World of God as a mystery; and he will continue in a material way of life.

Thou art brave.children. Thou hast set out on an unknown pilgrimage which seemeth long, but which hath indeed been short in comparison to the Great Days. Thou art brave, and the compensation of Holy Grace resteth upon thee. The cleansing thou hast experienced in the past weeks is to give thee courage on the pathway.

When thou sayest a thing now, thou shalt know it because thou hast experienced it. And when thou doest a thing, thou knowest it because thou doest it within the Light and Will of God.

Thou hast been in the deepest discipleship training in the night hours, and thou hast had mirrored to thy soul-light the thoughts and plans on which thy soul-action will come forth.

The journey which seemeth to be at the end is now at the true beginning. In the night hours and in the days ahead thou wilt be shown the highlights of the pattern and the knowing.

Remember, he who hath the integrity of his own soul is harmed not. And he who carrieth his light seeth always a way, and no place is too dangerous to walk. For he who is of God and of the angels hath his path made for his feet, and hath his heart's light ever before him.

Thou art in a corridor. The corridor hath

a turn. The turn bringeth thee into a broad place. Thou findest thyself with many people who, as thyself, find a new life; and in the new life thou findest the great answer to peace—the great answer to things not as people plan them, but as they are.

On February 7, 1953, the day of our departure from New York City, Ann Ree wrote the following words: "This is the end of the first part of the Caravan—one of the most beautiful spiritual events ever to occur to two people. God has been with us in each step of the way. It is our hearts' desire that those who receive our work will receive it even as we have received it. May they know that when we stood in the Light, they also stood in the Light with us. Each day has been interesting and vital and beautiful; each day the Masters' presence has been proved to us. We know that we have received more than we humanly deserved, for we have shared the beauty in the Masters' light; and now we come to a greater portal, that we may stand within the Garment of Jesus."

11
The Rugged Wonderfuls

And now, O Father, glorify thou me with thine own self with the glory which I had with thee before the world was.

—St. John 17:5

The golden lives of enlightened personages reflect the strength and splendor of truth and righteousness. The essence of their dedicated lives may be found wherever men desire to become pure, to worship God, and to learn of ethics and of Heaven. These master-builders and ambassadors for God link reverent men with the wisdom of the past and the spiritual theme of the present—and prepare men for the future.

When a woman has earned adept powers, and becomes a channel for the light of Heaven, she is known to the Higher Worlds as a "Fountain." Such women work quietly, humbly, and selflessly—giving freely of the refreshing waters of truth. Their only desire is to share with others that which God, in His bountifulness, has shared with them. Those who sent telepathic directives to Ann Ree sometimes called her "La Fonte"—the Fountain.

One night, during our return trip to Florida, Ann Ree and I decided to view the paintings we had completed in New York City. We studied one painting at a time in our stopping place. While looking at Ann Ree's painting, "Master R on an Island of Light," we saw two lines suddenly appear in the form of an X through Master R's body. The supernaturally imprinted lines became an indelible part of the painting. Ann Ree recognized the lines to be St. Andrew's cross—the X-shaped cross on which St. Andrew was crucified. She was later told inwardly that Master R is co-atom to St. Andrew, the disciple of Jesus.

In Florida, the morning and evening recording periods continued to be sacred times of communion with Heaven. A telepathic directive stated that the next phase of the Caravan would be called "the rugged wonderfuls."

Each day many pages were added to the manuscript files—pages containing important spiritual revealings. Ann Ree's one theme was "the eternal promise for man as a child and son of God."

Revelations relating to the plan in cosmos continued for two months after our return to Barjona. Then, April 1953, Ann Ree began to record hitherto unknown facts about Jesus and His disciples. She gave the background of humanity before the time of Jesus, and described the true purpose of Jesus and of His Messiah action in the earth. She disclosed the tie between John the Baptist and Jesus, and spoke of the great Saviour ideas. She told of other eternity systems in which Jesus had lived.

While working on the manuscript about Jesus, Ann Ree researched the prototypal story of man, and learned of the seven genesis levels in the human spirit. She stated that men are now expressing twelve prototypes, but that some persons of the earth will eventually achieve a thirteenth prototypal action, and become "like" Jesus (I John 3:1-3). Such persons will fulfill the *Jesus-man prototype.*

The manuscript pertaining to Jesus was accompanied by several charts and diagrams. One chart disclosed the thirteen *vortice-pools of worship.* This chart explained why there are so many different worship-paths to God.

In the spring of 1953 Ann Ree began a series of pastel paintings correlating to her manuscript. One of the paintings, titled "The Hour is Come" (St. John 17:1), showed Jesus to be co-atom to the Christ. A painting of Judas revealed the conflict between his compulsion to betray Jesus and his love for Jesus. In this painting Judas is surrounded by his personal angels who hold open the door to his contrition.

Judas now dwells in the eighth sphere *or "outer darkness" described by Jesus. Because Judas was contrite, he works now to raise the condemned from the lower regions of purgatory.*

The manuscript on Jesus also described the overall picture of present-day religions, stating their purposes, failures, and future. On April 9, 1953, Ann Ree received the following telepathy from the Hollander: "The major problem in religion today is confusion in the minds of men, and the justification of selfishness in holy places; the justification of separateness in holy issues; and the justification of man's procrastination on awaiting his salvation from without rather than from within.

"Religion has taught men that in gathering together they may be at one in a common purpose, and yet be separate as to the individual's reaching for Christ and God. But religion has not served the purpose of making clarity between man and God, and of making the Christ, the Son of God, clear to man in his consciousness. Religion now bears the karma of not having interpreted God and His Son to man; but, rather, having used the church as a means to personal gain and personal climb.

"Men now approach the time in which religion will meet its karma, and be sifted. And men's minds will begin to seek God in meditation."

In the latter part of April, Ann Ree composed a number of *Chantilly Prose-Poem Mantrams.* These mantrams correlated to certain initiations she was experiencing in the night during sleep.

The heart of the Chantilly forest in France is a mighty spiritual polarity. Between Easter and Pentecost the telepathic disciples and Cosmos Disciples meet at 3:00 A.M. in the etheric counterpart of the Chantilly forest.

CHANTILLY PROSE-POEM MANTRAM

Blessed art thou, young eagle who taketh thy flight.
Blessed art thou, O winged dove, bruised in flight.
Blessed art thou, O disciple, who seeth not but who hopeth.
Blessed art thou, each disciple.
The light of God's Love anointeth thee.

The glory of God is upon thee.
The power of thy fulfillment is in thee.
The might of the climb is with thee.
Disciple, rise in thy light; rise in thy love.
Disciple of the olden day, resign thyself to the new.
Disciple of the now, resign thy unknowing to instruction.
Disciple of the morrow, resign thyself to the work, and look thou not back.
Behold the glory of God.
Behold His Love.
Behold His Son.
Behold thy true self.
Behold thy will in God.
Meet that which faceth thee.
Kindle thy heart's love.
Forgive those who make an evil mystery of thy good.
All things come to him who singeth the song of Christ—
Who singeth the song of his soul.

In her first experiences with the greater archetypes, Ann Ree had learned that many solar systems have earth-like planets. She called these systems with earths, or terrestrial-type planets, "cosmic eternity systems." She saw that all forms of life now on earth have lived in other eternity systems in cosmos. She saw that Jesus had known His disciples in former earth or eternity systems; and that persons who truly follow Him today have also known Him and followed Him in other cosmic eternities. Jesus said, "My sheep hear my voice, and I know them, and they follow me" (St. John 10:27).

Ann Ree was shown that during the forming of the earth billions of souls were transported from dying solar systems into a virginal void. These souls were propelled into the new void through a mighty Light-Stream action. She saw that those who came into this earth or cosmic eternity system have the opportunity to develop a unique mentality or consciousness.

The archetypal revelation of the seven geneses was disclosed to Ann Ree. This revelation provided her with the key to understanding the different genesis levels in the human spirit. She saw that through palingenesis or reincarnation the individual proceeds from one level of genesis to another; and that it may take millions or even billions of years for many souls to evolve from *tribal-genesis* into *family-genesis*. Some will remain in tribal-genesis during the entire life of this planet, while others will rise more rapidly into the higher geneses.

Ann Ree saw that the seven geneses in the human spirit are: (1) tribal or nomadic-genesis; (2) family or human-genesis; (3) self-genesis; (4) cosmos-genesis; (5) pro-genesis; (6) all-genesis; (7) one-genesis. The following passages are excerpts from her writings on the seven geneses.

> Many in the world today are yet in tribal-genesis and human-genesis. However, in this present spiral of action, all men are stirring and seeking to rise into higher levels of evolvement.

Pure disciples are in the higher stages of self-genesis. The Cosmos Disciples have attained cosmos-genesis.

Persons who refuse to move beyond tribal-genesis or lesser family-genesis are *laggard souls.* When men reach the age of cosmos-genesis, these laggard ones will enter into a twilight sleep. This is the period when the "sheep" will be divided from the "goats." After the seventh Great Interval has concluded in this earth, all laggard souls will find themselves in other eternity systems suitable to their evolvement, where once more they will be given the opportunity to rise.

In the beginning of an eternity system all forms of life are first etheric. When the gravity of this earth reached its equilibrium, man's glandular system developed, and he began to produce offspring.

In tribal or nomadic-genesis, man's ideal is preservation of the tribe. Therefore he expresses his thinking, sentiently, through the sense-body of the tribe. In seeking to preserve the tribe, he develops his instinctual intelligence.

In family or human-genesis, man's ideal is preservation of the family. Thus he expresses his thinking, emotionally, through the emotions and feelings of the family. Family and blood relationships are repeatedly experienced until perfection is brought forth as to the ideal in the human association. It is the purpose of the family association that man acquire reverence.

When he has achieved reverence, he becomes an outstanding personality, and therefore helpful to humanity at large.

The personality is a product of the ages. The personality of each man is produced by the thread of both reverent and irreverent tribal and family associations through countless ages.

Self-genesis is divided into two parts. The first part is for the purpose of man's producing individuality; the second part is for the purpose of his producing selflessness. Whereas personality is produced from tribal and family association, individuality is produced from associating with persons outside the tribe or family. The unfamiliar and non-blood relatings work to produce individuality for man.

In lesser self-genesis, man becomes detached from the former family encasement, and seeks to blend with society rather than family. In this he loses the intimate love he formerly had for his family association. His action moves into the thought world, preponderantly intellect; his emotions are muted and inarticulate. The intellect being predominant, he becomes more critical in his attitude toward love and its demands upon him. He expresses wrong expectations toward love—expecting to be loved in spite of his critical mind and selfish actions. In his desire for individuality, he fails to fulfill the love-expectations of others. He develops strong guilt feelings due to certain unfulfilled family relationships, and a tremendous strain is placed upon the mental body, endangering his mental health.

In some rare instances, genius is manifested in the first part of self-genesis. In this, one has the danger of personalized egotism.

In one of the early phases of self-genesis, man's ideal is preservation of his right to think and act as an individual, and his right to explore every degree of life. From this phase of self-genesis has come the scientific age.

In certain earlier phases of self-genesis, there is a period in which the pendulum of man's temperament swings completely to the opposite of reverence. Thus he expresses irreverence for the proven things of the past. He attacks, and becomes antagonistic to, the decaying ideals centered in family or tribe. He seeks, intellectually, to preserve the ideal in self-discovery and experience. Irreverence and intellect become the critical mind. He despises historical inheritance, both religious and educational. He fortifies himself only through self-opinion. And he would lay to waste everything which has formerly produced the cultures of mankind. Out of this come revolutions in governments, separateness in families, upheavals in religions; and unreasoning prejudices are accentuated against races, creeds, and religions.

As man gradually evolves in self-genesis, his irreverence begins to be rationalized through certain fundamental laws; and the supporting truths of the universe become apparent to the higher logic within his thought world. The violent, hidden or open rebellion against tradition and its inheritance is tempered into a higher phase of reasoning, accompanied by a degree of reverence for the worthwhile attributes of man as to feeling and thinking. Out of this come the higher phases of self-genesis—the man in the world who would preserve an ideal which presents to man his right to feel reverently, to love selflessly, and his right to worship and find his God through direct relating of the heart to the mind.

In the second part of self-genesis, he begins to teach and impart instruction, showing what the ideal man can be, so that others in the world, in their relating to God, may seek to become the *ideal man.*

In the last part of self-genesis, one strives for impersonality rather than personality. His senses become soul-faculties. He uses the higher degrees of emotions and thought. And he strives for selfless serving and dedication, so that in the coming genesis, cosmos-genesis, he may become a Being and express through unobstructed mediation in alignment with the Christ Mind.

In higher self-genesis, the conflict and separateness within the family group are replaced by honoring and respecting the individuality of each member of the family. Love is expressed on a higher spiral. Such families consist of purer egos who, as catalyst associates, create within the rising spiral of evolutionary cultures.

The Old Testament is a true record of the transition process of man's rise from tribal-genesis to human-genesis. The New Testament contains the promise of man's spiritual potential in self-genesis, cosmos genesis, and pro-genesis.

Tribal-genesis and human-genesis had reached a decadent stage when Jesus came into the world. It is when these decaying periods are experienced in the earth that great Saviour action is made possible. In such a time came Jesus as Saviour and Messiah to give men "the way, the truth, and the life."

When Moses received the tablets of testimony on Mount Sinai, he destroyed the first tablets because people of the earth were not ready to receive them. The tablets he destroyed were the sapphire-blue tablets. These tablets contained the laws for higher human-genesis, self-genesis, and cosmos-genesis. Moses gave to the people the Ten Commandments, rather than the sapphire-blue tablets.

Jesus later activated the sapphire-blue tablets for men. These tablets pertain to the greater ethics and the Will of God. When men have finally incorporated the Ten Commandments into their emotions and thoughts, they will receive the sapphire-blue tablets, so that in the billions of years before them they may become as the sons of God.

Among other things, Jesus gave the laws for self-genesis and cosmos-genesis. After cosmos-genesis has been fulfilled, and men have reached pro-genesis, the Laws of God will be completely sealed into them and they will live within the Light rather than the law, for they will be "like" Jesus.

During the latter part of self-genesis, man is overshadowed by the twelve perfected disciple prototypes who were the disciples of Jesus in earth, and who now—co-atom to Jesus—dwell in the Realm of Light, or the Third Heaven. In this overshadowing, man begins the trials onto discipleship, preparing him for the coming cosmos-genesis.

The cosmos-genesis disciple works with the eternals, that he may reveal the mysteries within God.

John, the beloved disciple of Jesus, represents the pure, perfected prototype that men shall strive to emulate in the latter part of self-genesis and in the beginning of cosmos-genesis.

After cosmos-genesis, man will enter into pro-genesis. In pro-genesis he will fulfill the perfected Jesus-man prototype. Having produced a perfect mental body, and having acquired the pure love-ethic, he will blend with Jesus, the Christ, and the Father, fulfilling Jesus' saying, "At that day ye shall know that I am in my Father, and ye in me, and I in you" (St. John 14:20). This shall be the day of manifestation, and the beginning of the fulfillment of man's inheritance of the earth.

When men have reached the stage of pro-genesis, they shall do "greater works than these . . . " as promised by Jesus. They shall begin a hierarchy work in this earth, and they will use the constellation powers of manifestation and de-manifestation.

In all-genesis and one-genesis, men will increase their powers of manifestation and will become as the hierarchs.

> *Jesus answered them, Is it not written in your law, I said, Ye are gods?*
>
> —St. John 10:34

12
Wooded Place

He that hath my commandments, and keepeth them, he it is that loveth me: and he that loveth me shall be loved of my Father, and I will love him, and will manifest myself to him.

—St. John 14:21

In June 1953, Ann Ree mailed the manuscript for *Islands of Light* to a publisher friend in California. A few weeks later he said to her on the telephone, "It looks good. I would like to talk with you about it." We recognized this to be the time for the Caravan to move west.

After arriving in California, we learned that the publisher could not print the book for several months. However, we located another interested publisher, who accepted the book and began its printing immediately.

The two friends who had taken Ann Ree to the Great Sierras found a cabin for us in the mountains twenty miles north of Santa Barbara. Our Caravan name for the cabin was "Wooded Place." Here Ann Ree experienced her third archetypal illumination.

Line by line, page by page, as the Niscience formulas and ideas unfolded, it became apparent to Ann Ree that she was the recipient of a premeditated System from the Archetypal Worlds—a System that would meet the spiritual needs of the advanced disciples of this age, and of the coming age of scientific maturity.

We now stood upon the threshold of the realization of our hopes. The angels had watched over us in all things. The "loaves and the fishes" of the Lord were manifested each day.

The Wooded Place stood in a grove of twisted oaks. The environment was primitive, wild. Quail, deer, and hummingbirds moved about us as we worked in this mountain overlook.

The days were desert hot; the nights were cool and fragrant with Nature's healing pungencies. I learned to acclimate my body to the heat reflected from the pyramid-like, sepia-colored mountains.

We were busy and prayerful. The book Islands of Light *was in the press; we were now ready to see the tangible results of our previous work.*

In the mornings, at ten o'clock, we received the telepathic directives. Immediately afterward we applied ourselves to the banked recordings *pouring forth from my thoughts. The Niscience archetypal formulas and ideas came rapidly into my mind.*

There are certain disciples who have the power of telepathic induction. They are used by the Higher Worlds to ask salient and relevant questions of a telepathic disciple. From spiritually inspired questions, a banked recording is ignited in the mind of the telepathic disciple. Jonathan has this inductive grace. Our co-atom labors produced the System of Niscience.

Each morning we worked in a glide-swing under the great oaks behind the cabin. One day, while working on a new manuscript, I beheld the Lord Jesus. He suddenly appeared in front of a large oak tree. He was not clothed in etheric garments, but was clothed as He was in the world. As He spoke, He pointed to a mighty star slightly above me. The star moved toward me with a singing, humming tone. Never before had I experienced such intensity of light. The calm, beautiful words of Jesus steadied my thoughts. My reaction was one of divine rapture and grandeur. Falling from the star were three drops of crimson blood. Jesus said, "This is your own direct star. You have come under your own direct star." I saw that the three drops of blood pertained to three former lives in which I had experienced martyrdom—and I knew that I had become co-atom to Jesus. He showed me that one who brings the archetypal light must unite with the star from whence he comes—a star far out in cosmos. He said that the memory from this former eternal day was now being quickened in my soul.

When one makes alignment with his direct star, he no longer thinks of himself and the preservation of his body, or the preservation of human objects and possessions. From the time he unites with his direct star he is caught into God's mighty momentum.

From the moment that Jesus appeared to me at Wooded Place, I have had no time to waste; I have had nothing that belonged to me; I have had only that which was for the Niscience I was bringing forth.

After my vision of Jesus and the direct star, each remaining mosaic portion of the Niscience system coalesced and merged. I saw how scientific men, in releasing the atom-wisdom to the world, had opened with one mighty gesture the dynamics of energy within energy. Slowly, men would begin to study, read, and apply their Scriptures with another dimension of insight. The minds of men in the scientific age would unveil the spiritual allegories.

I saw that Jesus had timed His birth two thousand years before the scientific age for a specific reason. He had planted His seed-truths of everlasting life so that men might reap their harvest in the scientific age. Jesus foresaw that men in the scientific age would at last understand intellectually the transubstantiation powers within energy and light—and thus, through repeated research and revelation, would cross the barrier of unknowing into knowing.

During her experience with Jesus, Ann Ree repeated His words to me as she heard them. However, I could not write the words, for even the slight noise of a pencil's movement on paper seemed to be an irreverent intrusion upon the sacredness of the moment. In addition to His words about her direct star, He also told her that men were as sheep who needed Commandments to shepherd and guide them—and that there would be a day when men would no longer need Commandments.

Ann Ree, inspired by her experience with Jesus, composed the following mantram:

Peace unto all men.
Blessings be upon all men.
Let all men come unto the Christ.
Let all men know Him and receive Him.
At dusk as we stand in the Garment of
the Jesus One,

May we know His healing and forgiving love.
And may we place our cares unto Him,
And go forth unto the world
To heal,
To serve.

In a morning telepathic directive Ann Ree was told that one of the means by which she would be able to identify persons who were prepared for the new System and its blueprint for discipleship was by their response to the mantrams.

After the Ancient of Days appeared to her in 1949, Ann Ree became increasingly aware of the importance of "timing" in the physical life and in the spiritual life. She learned of the spiritual tides of light that revivify the souls of men during certain periods of the day and the night. Her knowledge of these tides was incorporated into the spiritual practices within the System of Niscience.

When the soul of man becomes diamond-like, the facets of his soul become a prism-hourglass for the Christ. Man's timing and his grace become as one. He responds to the spiritual tides of Heaven—and all who stand near him come under the mantle of his grace.

All persons have grace, but not all are free to use the assets of their grace. To free one's grace, one should revere God, and make a covenant to qualify himself to fulfill the law of timing. He begins by seeing God's equation working within all events.

If one fulfills his smallest and most menial tasks with diligence and with joy; if he fulfills his promises to himself and to others—he will come into timing, and he will reap the greater benefits of his grace. He will become not only a diligent and trustworthy person, but he will come under the guidance and supervision of the Holy Presences of Heaven; for he will have made himself a worthy timekeeper for Heaven.

When one has opened his spiritual grace, he reverently anticipates the spiritual tides. Not all persons respond to the same spiritual tides. Some feel the need to commune with God during the spiritual tide in the early morning; some in the noon day; some at dusk; and an increasing number of persons unite themselves with the spiritual tide occurring at 11:00 P.M. The spiritual tide at 11:00 P.M. is the period in which earth-initiates receive a unique rejuvenation and instruction.

Those who are completely engrossed in their physical activities of the day are unaware of the spiritual tides. However, while sleeping, their souls respond in some degree to the spiritual tides of the night.

Anyone who fulfills a continuity in spiritual serving intuitively responds to each spiritual tide in its sequence. If a person has the grace to respond to all of the tides, he has a fluidic cognizance and a range of action beyond the average individual. The resuscitating helps of these spiritual tides reinforce his labors, and give a spiritual vigor to his serving.

The spiritual tide occurring at sunrise is a tide of animation and quickening. Those who respond to the spiritual tide at sunrise often become ambassadors for the light of Heaven; their souls' prompting stirs them to awake and unite with all waking and stirring life of the earth. One whose timing is alerted to this hour experiences within himself a mediative current of exquisite peace and upliftment. He unites himself with Heaven's design, and he sees men arising from their sleep as creators in a fertile world.

One who regularly awakens after *the spiritual tide of sunrise may unite his thoughts with the instruction received from his soul during the night's sleep.*

Ten o'clock in the morning is a propitious time for dedication, because in this hour the soul reminds one that he is a creator. The spiritual tide of 10:00 A.M. stirs the intellect. The tasks of the day are clarified, and one may coordinate his emotions with a hidden strength to meet the day's demands.

The spiritual tide at twelve noon enables one to contemplate the magnanimities of Heaven. At noon, man's wonder-consciousness and his naïvete are at their height; there is a hushed moment in which he may be free of harsh judgments toward his fellow man. He may use the meridian powers of the noon sun to conjoin his prayers with the prayers of the Mother of the World. At the exact moment of noon each day the Mother of the World places her garment of forgiveness over the erring ways of men. All the powers of forgiving in Heaven are fused; the angels, the Saints, and the Holy Presences of Heaven experience a rapture of union with eternal good—and they envision man as he is to be.

The lesser etheric body ceases to respond to the influence of the physical sun at 3:30 in the afternoon, and begins to respond to the lunar rays. This transition from the solar to the lunar rays affects the emotions of man, and enables the soul to come closer to his mind.

From 3:30 P.M. to the time of the dusk spiritual tide one moves closer to his conscience. If he inwardly feels that he has fallen short of his creative aims, he is weary and discontented. His egotism is at its lowest ebb, and thus he is more likely to respond to the spiritual tide at dusk. When one's thoughts are retrospective, and he reflects upon his actions and motives of the daytime hours, he has the opportunity to gain a deeper perspective and insight into his motives; for in the dusk time his individual will is less forceful. If one is highly evolved, he feels a humility and a self-inadequacy. The demotion of self makes it possible for him to turn to the greater help received from the Lord Jesus during the spiritual tide at dusk. In the violet dusk of the sunset hour, the Lord Jesus comes closer to men; and those, who will, may see themselves through the perspective of Heaven. At sunset or dusk the curtain rises upon the spiritual life of man, and the Lord Jesus, the Sovereign of the human spirit, moves tenderly and closely into the open hearts of those who lift up their prayers at day's ending.

In the world there are certain anointed ones who have given themselves over to the very special mission of healing the wounds inflicted by charlatanism and exploitation. These anointed ones, understanding the law of transposing one current into another, work to overcome the psychical tumults which are rampant at 9:00 P.M.

Each night at eleven o'clock the molten sea within the earth, the axis of the earth, and the innermost point of the Kingdom of God are united. This heavenly conjoining is called the fulcrum hour. *A mighty upsurge of spiritual power is generated in Heaven and in earth—touching all living organisms, sentient beings, and degrees of consciousness. The sum total of the evil consummated in the day just past is mitigated. Thus, evil can never become victor in the world. Evil will ultimately be replaced with good.*

Those who respond to the eleven o'clock spiritual tide work with the momentum of the fulcrum action. If they have the power to witness the fulcrum action, they see that the earth is enveloped by a mighty network or medallion, and that at each point of the medallion there stands a spiritual sentinel or holy presence. From 11:55 until twelve midnight the highest point of illuminative light exists in Heaven and in earth—and the upsurge of the fulcrum action culminates in a world-purging, cleansing, healing.

There is a tryst tide before the early dawn of each rising day. This occurs at 3:00 A.M. Advanced disciples, telepathic disciples, and Cosmos Disciples meet in the etheric realms where they work for the peace of the nations and continents.

In Florida, Ann Ree had seen a vision of a golf course with oil wells, and she predicted that some day we would play on this course. Several months later in California, while living at Wooded Place, we drove to Santa Maria to play golf. When we saw oil wells busily at work on the beautiful golf course, we immediately recalled her vision and prophecy.

Walking has always been Ann Ree's main form

of exercise. The game of golf enabled her to walk on the natural earth, and to enjoy what she called "a metaphysical game." At other times, she would take a "creative or mediative walk."

A creative walk is a walk during which one feels a great opening of beauty within the day. The mountains, the trees, the sky—all appear as a new canvas for the Hand of God.

A mediative walk is one in which the person is a mediative instrument for his community. He starts his walk loaded down with the riches of Heaven, and he disperses them one by one into the various areas of the community.

After *Islands of Light* was published, Ann Ree gave a lecture in downtown Los Angeles. When the talk was over—and the visitors and guests had departed—she sat down at a piano and played for several minutes. I was surprised to learn that she had never received formal instruction, for she played effortlessly and beautifully. She told me that even in her childhood years she enjoyed "making up" songs on the piano. Later in her life, this talent became the ability to play the themes and melodies that she heard inwardly.

The manuscript on Jesus written by Ann Ree in Florida touched upon *etheric anatomy* and the eternal atoms within the everlasting body. The manuscript she recorded at Wooded Place contained a comprehensive description of the eternal or spiritual atoms of man. The following passages are excerpts from her discoveries about the spiritual atoms.

> The spiritual atoms of man are deathless portions of life, image, and light. The spiritual

atoms remain eternal in all worlds, and are the means of sustaining the physical experiences on earth and the spiritual experience in the World of God. These atoms are not the atoms of force; nor are they organic. They are atoms of the pure stream of the eternals, and consist wholly of light and of the body of God. They make up the fabric of man's interweaving and intermeshing—a network of life, image, and light, enabling man to function in the world of form, and still have entrance into the World of God.

Man's spiritual evolvement is yet in the embryonic stage. This earth is the womb for his coming forth. Jesus of Nazareth is the ideal prototype or blueprint of the perfect man. Previous to entering this eternity, Jesus had command of the twelve atoms in each of His four bodies. Thus, He had the power of manifestation and de-manifestation. Through this power He was able to change one substance into another (water into wine), to multiply substance (fishes and loaves), to heal the sick, to change one energy into another, to disappear and appear, to command the elements, to walk on water, to raise the dead, and to teach of the everlasting Kingdom of God. Being a firsthand witness of the Kingdom of God, He could instruct men as to Heaven's reality.

The higher etheric body or everlasting body of man consists of twelve eternal atoms, which remain unchangeable—retaining their original eternal relation to one another. The average man must work for aeons to perfect the atoms in his physical body, emotional body, and mental body.

In the present age, man's physical body contains nine orifice atoms, correlating to the nine orifices or openings of the physical body.

The emotional body atoms of man are now the determining factor as to his evolvement. Some in earth have evolved only the five lesser or sentient atoms of the emotional body; others have evolved seven, and, in some rare instances, ten. In the emotional body may always be found one atom which is *individualistic*. During certain intervals, this individualistic atom becomes an agitator to the atoms within the physical, emotional, and mental bodies. Through this agitation, man is initiated into a greater degree of consciousness.

If a person has but five sentient atoms activated in his emotional body, the agitation caused by the individualistic atom will result in some form of violence to, or suffering in, the physical body; some form of emotional tension in the emotional body; and some form of disturbance in the thoughts. Such pain and suffering refines the senses and makes them better instruments for the soul. If a person has activated seven emotional body atoms, the individualistic atom

works upon the physical, emotional, and mental bodies to make each body a better vehicle or instrument, so that one may work more directly with his soul. If a person has activated ten emotional body atoms, the individualistic atom produces a heavenly recognition of him as a personage or a holy presence in Heaven and on earth. The individualistic atom in the emotional body of the holy person enables him to return to the earth if he so desires, or if there is need for his presence on earth.

Until man has activated twelve atoms in each body, the individualistic atom will continue to agitate, stimulate, and stir the other atoms in the various bodies. The purpose of the individualistic atom is to make man aware of his eternal identity and of his soul and Heaven. As long as the individualistic atom is active, there is heavenly hope that man will seek a way out of materialistic and sensual expression.

Each person, upon entry into this eternity system, quickened three mental atoms in his mental body. Regardless of the degree of his evolvement, each person of this earth has three mental body atoms: (1) the supreme-will atom; (2) the imaging atom; and (3) the eternal-light atom.

The *supreme-will atom* of the mental body relates man to the Will of God. The *imaging atom* of the mental body relates him to the Father. The *eternal-light atom* of the mental body relates him to the Christ and to the greater archetypes under command of the Christ.

Through many initiations and spiritual advancements, some persons will gain mastery of the three mental body atoms, and thus will free the nine dormant atoms of the mental body. Others of the earth, being in love with the physical life and their physical selves, will be unable to coordinate and master the three mental body atoms; when this earth eternity system has concluded, such persons will be compelled to undergo initiations in other eternity systems until they have total command of the three mental body atoms.

Until man has total command of the supreme-will atom of the mental body, and is at one with the Will of God; until he has mastered the power of imaging selflessly; until he has the power of revelation through the eternal-light atom, relating him to the Christ—his thoughts will be concerned more with his self-interest, his emotions will be used for self-preservation, and his creative works will be concerned solely with self-aggrandizement in the world. When the supreme-will atom, the imaging atom, and the eternal-light atom are in perfect alignment, man will no longer seek to preserve himself; he will work directly with the Will of God, with the imaging power of the Father, and with the archetypal light of the Christ.

One can best determine his own degree of mental evolvement by observing the predominant theme of his thinking. If his thoughts are saturated with self-will and the desire to gain for himself, he is using the lower aspect of the supreme-will atom of the mental body; but if his thoughts are filled with the will to do the good, the pure and the real, he is preparing to come under the guidance of the Will of God.

If one is using the slower rhythms of the imaging atom, he will think traditional thoughts; he will be satisfied to conform to the thoughts of the masses. However, if he is highly evolved as a vessel for humanity, he will become at one with the Father; and the pure stream of imaging will enter into his thoughts.

If one desires truth, and has the courage to envision the new spiritual transitions, he is influenced by his eternal-light atom correlating to the Christ. If one has an inquiring mind—and lacks reverence for the minds of others—he will appoint himself as a messiah over others. But if he has gained the spiritual insight throughout the ages, he will pursue Light as a spiritual neophyte or acolyte; he will aspire to be illumined in Christ. The eternal-light atom will unite him with the greater archetypes, and he will come under the tutelage of the Christ-Spirit.

When a holy person thinks, the supreme-will atom, the imaging atom, and the eternal-light atom are coordinated—and his thoughts are creative, fulfilling the perfect equation in thought.

The atoms within the higher etheric body enable the atoms in the physical body, the emotional body, and the mental body to penetrate, to fortify, and to influence one another.

In each body there are progressive atoms, or

atoms which have been quickened throughout the ages into progressive states. These atoms work more freely with the higher etheric body. Until the time of Jesus, the progressive atoms were used for survival. The resurrection of Jesus began a quickening of a higher degree of atom progression in the humanities. After the coming of Jesus, those who truly followed His precepts experienced a quickening within the *indestructible atom* in their foreheads. Such enlightened ones began to stir other atoms within their bodies, and to learn more about their spiritual natures and the Spiritual Worlds.

Many in the world are yet content to express sensuality through the five sentient atoms in the lesser emotional body. When one has reached spiritual maturity, his sentient atoms no longer command him; the sentient atoms are stilled within the lesser emotional body—and his soul-faculties are freed. He produces a quickened intuition, rather than instinctual sensing. His appetites become more selective, his charity more expansive. His eye beholds the souls of men; he hears the greater harmonies of the universe. He loves all things and all creatures of the earth; and he devotes himself to God with his heart, mind, and soul.

Prayer makes pure the oil in the lamps of the senses, and the soul-faculties are free to give forth a pure light. Through meditation, the senses become the servants for the soul, fulfilling Jesus' parable of the "ten virgins" (St. Matthew

25: 1-13). The five sentient atoms in the lesser emotional body may be likened to the five foolish virgins; the soul-faculties working through the five higher emotional body atoms may be compared to the five wise virgins.

The spiritual hope for man is that the eternal work of God is endless within him. One by one, all atoms in their progressive, spiraling state will be set into alignment with the atoms of the higher etheric body, and therefore into the perfect light.

Meditation is the greatest power in the overcoming of human karma. Pure meditation, however, is impossible without *atom alignment.* When one is out of alignment with his spiritual  atoms, his thoughts and feelings during meditation are colored by personal uncertainties and desires.

When one has mastered the spiritual art of meditation, the higher self dwelling within the eternal sustaining atom speaks into the soul and into the mind—and one learns of the many processes and facets of the eternals. He no longer resists the great laws governing pain and joy on earth, and understands them to be a necessity in man's emotional and mental evolvement.

When the spiritual atoms are free, the higher self is free—and one becomes an heir to the promises of the Beatitudes, or Sermon on the Mount, as given by Jesus of Nazareth.

The planets, the earth, and the sun of this eternity system form a mathematical polarity through which the Spirit of God works. The sun, the earth, and the accompanying planets are encased in a mighty spiritual atom, called the *World-Soul Atom,* or *Diamond of the Ages.*

Each thing in the earth—from plant to man—has an *eternal sustaining atom.* Each eternal sustaining atom has a degree of light correlating to the Will, Life, Light, and Love of God. The degree of light within an eternal sustaining atom determines the form it will manifest and express, and also determines what it will contribute to the universal plan.

In the beginning of this eternity the Hierarchy dwelling within adjacent constellations, and our Father of this eternity, sounded Life-tones into the world-soul atom. These Life-tones played upon the eternal sustaining atoms dwelling in the cosmic mist of the yet unformed earth. As the earth became a coagulated body or mass, the four latent bodies within the eternal sustaining atom of man began to shape in vapor-like forms.

In man's eternal sustaining atom there is a soul-pulsation. The soul's pulsation, working with the Life-tones, quickened the sentient atoms within the emotional body. Next, nine physical body atoms were quickened; and following this, three mental body atoms were quickened.

The Life-tones of Hierarchy and the Father will continue to play upon the bodies of men until men have reached a state of perfection in this earth. As men evolve, the latent atoms in their various bodies will come forth.

With the coming of Jesus, the Christ Light-tones began for this eternity. When the Christ Light-tones penetrated the earth system, there began a coalescing between the Life-tones of the Father and Hierarchy, and the Light-tones of the Christ. When the Life-tones and the Light-tones converged, man began his long upward climb toward a perfected mentality. As the Light-tones of the Christ continue to move upon men, men will become more and more noble in their thoughts; and their minds will become vortices of creation.

In cosmos-genesis, man will have command of his emotional body atoms, and perfect control of his mental atoms. He will think, knowing the origin of thought, determining the measure by which he thinks, and the result of what he thinks. When this has come, man will have acquired the *omniscient cell* within the brain, and will use the power of Niscience, or that of knowing beyond knowledge.

13

Handful of God

He that receiveth a prophet in the name of a prophet shall receive a prophet's reward; and he that receiveth a righteous man in the name of a righteous man shall receive a righteous man's reward.

—St. Matthew 10:41

The Caravan moved from Wooded Place to Los Angeles in November 1953. Ann Ree spoke in public each Sunday, but those who first attended her talks had difficulty in understanding the new System. On July 16, 1952, while in Florida, Ann Ree had seen the name "Williams" in a vision. The vision was accompanied by the words: "The bringing forth of the strong; the running of the race; the gaining of the goal . . . " In January 1954, Ann Ree was giving a lecture in Los Angeles when the one with the name Williams appeared—the promised catalyst who was responsible for introducing a nucleus of strong disciples to the System of Niscience.

During the following months and years, ready students learned of Niscience and responded to the hum of the Niscience Archetype. Some of these ready ones recognized Ann Ree from visions they had had of her before actually meeting her—one had heard her name in a dream several months before Ann Ree came to California. Others recognized her as their teacher by her eyes, or her voice, or her answers to their questions, or by the spiritual love that emanated from her.

Several students saw meditative visions of the telepathic symbols of Fleur de Lis or the Hollander. When they described these symbols to Ann Ree, she knew that they had come under the blessing of the Niscience Archetype. In one instance a student accurately described Fleur de Lis and the outside of his home.

Those who responded to the Niscience Archetype realized that Ann Ree held the answers to their many questions. Gradually they began to understand her new terminology and archetypal revelations. Grace healings began to be manifested. The lives of these ready students were transformed; certain ones activated new spiritual gifts and talents. It warmed Ann Ree's heart to see the Niscience students evolve "a spiritual mellowness, devotion, and reverence."

In California we learned of many metaphysical cliques and groups. The majority of persons in these groups lacked reverence and discipline. Each group felt that it had the total answer to the religious and metaphysical life. Ann Ree's knowledge of the thirteen vortice-pools of worship enabled her to understand the necessity for different levels of religious and metaphysical instruction. She taught charitableness toward all religious, metaphysical, and spiritual teachings; however, she remained firm in her aversion to psychical exploitation and occult manipulation.

I was unable to accept the path of metaphysics,

occultism, or esotericism as being the complete path. As I advanced in my spiritual understanding, I turned more and more to the Christ—knowing that other ways, while containing certain truths, were for mental power and the development of the individuality, rather than for the power of the soul. Teachings devoid of the Christ were man-made columns in the outer court-yards of the spiritual Holy of Holies. The center or innermost arc of the spiritual temple is supported by the Christ.

God's World is a World of order. His World is not a vacuum; it is filled with innumerable Presences who seek at all times to bring Heaven closer to men.

I have never had a prayer go unanswered. And I have striven to pray not repetitiously or to ask for anything which would better my lot. I have prayed that I might be a channel of grace.

Prophets are ignored in this age because men are too dazzled with experimentation to receive their message.

I prayed for a handful of God. *God sent them to me. From the beginning, they were my heart-children, my spiritual daughters and sons.*

Throughout my life I have had a human-spirit love for people of all faiths and races. Many of these persons have preserved me and protected me. My grace-friends in the world are many. However, until the System of Niscience, I depended upon the Holy Presences of Heaven for sacred companionship. After Niscience was established, I found spiritual companions in the world who fulfilled the hope of my heart.

One by one they came. I recognized them by the "light in their foreheads." I knew that God's timing had showered His grace upon me as a prophet and a teacher.

The Ann Ree Colton Foundation of Niscience, a nonprofit Foundation, was established on November 25, 1953. Thus began the mediative Lay Ministry of Niscience, with its devotional sanctuaries and research units.

The intimate association in a small sanctuary fulfills the need to express a pure Christian ministry. The services are sacredly reverent, and the close association makes possible a spiritual proximity as expressed in the three hundred years after the death of Jesus.

The Caravan visited Sarasota, Florida from March to June 1954. Ann Ree named our Sarasota abode "Circle in the Sun." Here, she painted five of her past lives and united herself with the soul-grace from these lives. Some of her former students gathered around her for instruction—and to make the System of Niscience more understandable to them, she prepared her first "white paper" lessons. While in Sarasota, Ann Ree worked on a book about the life of Ikhnaton. She also began to formulate a manuscript concerning the time of Constantine, when the teaching of reincarnation was deleted from the Christian Church.

In the medieval times men were burned at the stake for their scientific discoveries; those having mystical visions were also martyred. The anathema or curse placed upon the belief in palingenesis or reincarnation by the Church Council in the sixth century determined the fate of the Christian multitudes and their worship;

for the Church became merely a vessel for the lesser mysteries rather than for the greater mysteries.

There are many persons in the world who seek to go beyond the lesser mysteries. Such persons know there is a greater ministry. They yearn to hear the spiritual word spoken by illuminative tongues.

On November 1, 1956, in Glendale, California, Ann Ree formed the Guild of Ethics, which became the core-strength for the teaching of the System of Niscience. In her research into the cloisters of Heaven and the heavenly sacraments accompanying worship, Ann Ree learned that a spiritual teaching, to fully express the Christ, should have seven arterial outlets:

1. Pure ethical instruction under the direction of dedicated teachers.
2. For children and adults, sanctuaries for reverent worship and devotion.
3. Instruction in the creative arts for the clarification of the soul-faculties.
4. Small units for
   (a) the sharing in meditation
   (b) training in the Lay Ministry
   (c) research into spiritual subjects as related to serving in the world
   (d) training in the art of spiritual logos or speaking, whereby the student may unite himself with the power of the Holy Ghost.
5. A proven body of disciples who meet once a month in guild or conclave action to align themselves with the mediation filigree of the Holy Presences of Heaven, so that they may

research the ethics in the spiritual life, and thereby extend the orbit of a healing ministry.

6. Written material containing daily spiritual exercises and instruction, and also instruction to enable the student to research his dreams and to extend his Night Ministry labors.

7. (a) The uniting with the Recording Angels upholding the structure of the Holy Bible, so that the student may research and extract the eternal wisdom and pure truths within the Bible

   (b) a study of the Jesus Ethic

   (c) open forums to circulate and to spread the benevolent and spiritual theme provided by the teaching.

In 1958 Ann Ree wrote *Draughts of Remembrance.* This lucid book on reincarnation was the result of her research into the souls and intimate lives of thousands of persons. *Draughts of Remembrance* has proved to be a spiritual treasure for persons of many faiths.

During the summer of 1958, Ann Ree suffered her first heart attack. A few days later she saw a vision of mothers looking toward Heaven. The vision was accompanied by these words:

And behold, I saw
A goodly company of women,
Their faces upturned unto the light.
Eye to eye they looked unto the eyes of
the angels,
The angels of the light,

The angels of birth and death,
The angels of guidance and patience.
In their faces I saw motherhood.
Crosses and trials
Had been erased from their faces.
And their eyes, luminous, looked upward,
For they stood under the blessing of Heaven.
And they gathered their young into their arms,
to their hearts—
Some at the level of their knees,
Some in their arms,
And some eye to eye.
All of these they had borne.
And all of these they looked to
As sons of God to come.
These are the true, pure mothers in the world.

In October 1958, while painting the design for a mosaic mural of the Holy Family, Ann Ree had a two-day illumination and uniting with the human spirit. During these days (in La Jolla, California), she suffered great sorrow for the humanities of the world. Her tears were co-mingled with the tears of all who weep in the world. The human-spirit initiation began by her seeing those who had been recently martyred; the innocent face of Anne Frank came before her eyes. She saw the blind bestiality of men who persecute the innocent, and she prayed for those who had perverted their wills and had become hostile agents for the principalities and powers of darkness.

The human spirit is indomitable and immortal. The human spirit is the combined soul of humanity through which the Father and His angels work. Regardless of how much it is tried and persecuted by the principalities and powers of darkness, the human spirit will thrive and prevail.

After her experience with the human spirit, Ann Ree composed the following mantram:

May the protective garment of the Holy
Presences
And the healing garment of the Ministering
Angels
Enfold and sustain
The young, the tender, and the helpless of the
earth.
And may each child of the earth lose not his joy.

The thousands of beautiful mantrams written by Ann Ree were received from the level of her soul-grace. She also composed many melodious anthems. These anthems came to her while she played the organ inspirationally, and were sometimes accompanied by mantramic words:

O Lord, the fragrance of Thy Spirit
Giveth unto me humility.
Thy fragrance is my anointing grace,
Saturating my callousness,
Giving perfection to my works of good,
And undoing my works of error and negation.
O Lord, let Thy holy fragrance anoint me again
and again,

Until I be free and wholly in the state of love
For my fellow man.

* *

Into my soul
There comes
A light,
A light of hope.
Into my heart
There comes
A warming way.
The gate long closed
Now opens
Unto me.
I stand
In a new vista
Of hope, of love.
In my soul
I am never defeated.
My heart
Is a struggling
Channel
And instrument.
My soul
Is a vessel
Of golden
Perfection,
And is undefeatable.

The following telepathic directive was received by Ann Ree one morning in 1959: "The peace of pure joy is thy habitation. A beloved presence of the angels goeth with thee, anointing thy way and making sacred the happenings on the way. Look thou for the sacred signals and happenings on the way. And place thy hands, thy heart, and thy thoughts into total guidance on the way, for the Guardians of the Spiritual Worlds work best when thou dost place thy total faith, thy complete faith, in guidance on the way. In that which thou doest with thy heart, thy hands, and thy mind, place thyself in trust on God's destination, God's journey for thee—for thou hast set upon a journey for God."

In her twenty-fifth year Ann Ree had seen a dream-vision in which she was shown a panorama of the years before her. She was told that at the ending of her days she would be surrounded by many children. This has proven to be true, for a constant source of joy to her in the establishing of Niscience has been her work with children and young adults. She has a very special gift which enables her to see into the hearts of children. Some of the most beautiful testimonies of her work have come from grateful parents.

On the Sunday night after the June solstice of 1960, Ann Ree received her second blessing from Mary, the mother of Jesus.

In a dream, Mary showed me that she works with the Mother of the World. Mary's blue, gold and opalescent veil surrounded me and covered me. I felt her healing and anointing love—and these words poured from her veil, "Be pure and teach the pure."

As part of the System of Niscience, Ann Ree provides her students with the *etheric code* to visions and dreams. In this instruction she gives each student a way in which he may understand the difference between the spiritual symbols of the soul and the psychical, primitive symbologies.

Few people recognize where the psychical ends and the spiritual begins. Through visions and dreams one can gauge whether he is living in a psychical state or in a spiritual state. The only way that dreams and visions can become linguistic to one is through the understanding of the etheric code correlating to the master symbols in the archetypal realms.

All persons have psychical powers. As long as one remains irreverent toward the spiritual nuances within the universe, he will continue to express the crude, electrical, psychical energies in his emotions and thoughts. His dream world will be colored with lust, sensuousness, and self-reproach.

The psychical power is similar to a current of raw electricity. It has the power to bring disquiet, to disturb the peace.

When men are all intellect, they use the psychical power in their cunning wills. When men are emotionally immature, they use psychical power to intrude where angels fear to tread.

As the mentality and the emotions of men come to balance, spiritual nature comes to birth. The spiritual nature harnesses the psychical power and keeps it under control.

Spiritual nature in man sees his mind as a creative instrument for God, and reveres creative thinking, knowing its source to be from God, the One.

The heart-man of pure emotions is a devotee of the Christ, a humanitarian for man; his love is used to heal the wounds inflicted upon the human spirit.

For years I had observed that there was no existing school of ethics as to the use of spiritual knowledge and the interpretation of visions and dreams.

When I began to receive the archetypal revelations, the code-symbols I had used previously in my ministry to interpret visions and dreams were extended. The dream worlds of my students were laid open to me. I received a Joseph mantle *to interpret dreams.*

Sleep, to some persons, is a form of anesthesia or a means of escape and forgetfulness; but to others it is a recovery and awakening to a greater sphere of consciousness. Sleep may become a creative labor within the night, in which a person may unite himself with the blueprint of God's intent for him.

The soul works without weariness to enable all persons to extend and broaden their states of consciousness during the hours of the day and the hours of sleep. The vocabulary or language of the soul is symbology. This language of symbology is more frequently experienced in the dream world during the night's sleep. When the senses are totally stilled during sleep, the soul seeks to mirror pure, mediative instruction. However, when one is worried, anxious or frustrated, the senses are magnified in the dream world—and the mediative instruction of the soul is sealed away.

All dreams are of vital importance to persons who desire to evolve spiritually. The spiritual student should look upon each dream experience as part of a sacred action overdirected by the work of the soul. In time he will come to understand the initiatory phases within dreams, and comprehend the etheric code within dream symbology and dream experience. Thus, he will be enabled to better understand his physical, emotional, and mental impulses—and also the hidden cause directing and stimulating his attitudes and actions in the world.

When a person is deeply engrossed with physical concerns, he rarely understands the true significance of dreams and the part dreams play as related to the soul. The average person is yet to recognize the soul's action in dreams, and either ignores his dreams or leans in the direction of the Freudian interpretation of dreams. The superstitious person fears his dreams. Few in the world relate themselves, intelligently and constructively, to that which the soul is seeking to reveal through dreams. Even those who intuit that dreams are spiritually significant are seldom qualified to fully interpret the etheric code concealed within dream symbology. To achieve a closer intimacy with the higher reaches of the soul's action, while either asleep or awake, requires a rhythmic and uninterrupted training; and also an inner perception which may be gained only through purification and dedication to God. Reverent dedication, earnest and repeated prayer, pure alignment in meditation, selfless contemplation, the speaking of mantrams, and certain periods of dedicated fasting will (1) extend and sustain the time spent in the higher realms of the dream world, (2) assure the retention of memory of dream dramas, (3) disclose the meaning within the dream drama, and (4) enable the student, in time, to coordinate his soul's action of the night with his physical labors and creative works of the day.

There are seven dream veils. The lowest or first dream veil envelopes the grotesque level of dreams. This veil correlates to the atavistic repressions dwelling within the primitive brain situated at the base of the skull.

The second dream veil, or level of fantasy, correlates to the psychic brain in the solar plexus. When one dreams on this level, he has fantastic hallucinations similar to those caused by high fevers.

The third dream veil, called the wish level, correlates to the frontal part of the brain and to the imagination. In these dreams a person pictures his unrequited yearnings. He often awakens from this dream state with a feeling of refreshing hopefulness.

The fourth dream veil relates to the akasic records, the records of things which have occurred in the earth, and to one's own soul records of past lives. The fourth dream veil is usually experienced in color, and sometimes music is in the background. When one opens this dream veil, he has begun to come closer to his soul; his soul is trying to teach him of the eternal and everlasting verities.

The fifth dream veil relates to certain evaluation trials in which the soul and one's Guardian Angel assist the one dreaming to open himself to the hidden motives within his nature or temperament—motives which stand between him and his soul. When he penetrates this dream veil, he undergoes a series of initiations. The first relates to his attitude toward sex; the second, his attitude toward money; the third, his attitude toward persons; the fourth, his attitude toward death; in the fifth, he researches his creative assets; in the sixth, he is initiated into the use of his spiritual ethic; in the seventh initiation, he becomes aware of the Risen Dead, the Saints, and certain Holy Presences.

When one penetrates the sixth dream veil, he becomes a Night-Ministry server. He also unites himself with the prophetic aspect of dreaming; thus, in the daytime he is very close to the guidance and overdirection of his soul.

The seventh dream veil may only be reached through spiritual grace. In this level of dreaming one comes close to the Holy of Holies. To reach the seventh level, one must be at peace with his conscience, with his faith in God. In the night hours of sleep he incorporates into himself the essences of wisdom which become, in daytime action, a blessing and anointing.

In a talk given in San Diego, California, Ann Ree made the following comments:

> Dreams are filled with symbolic stories. When one knows how to interpret dreams, he understands where he is spiritually, and where he is in his evolvement.
>
> Symbols are the language of the soul. Dream symbols, especially, are the language of the soul. Poetry is a language of the soul. All poetry is overdirected by the Cherubim Angels—and dreams have a certain poetic essence.
>
> Dreams sometimes have a prophetic theme, and they often have a corrective theme.

Ann Ree gives this advice to her students: "If one keeps a dream diary, he will be benefited beyond his expectations. When he researches his dream diary at the end of each month, he will begin to observe what his soul is saying to him."

The following dreams, interpreted by Ann Ree, are from the dream diary of Jonathan Murro:

In a dream I saw a large table shaped in the form of a "W." Hundreds of men and women of dignified appearance and noble character were sitting around the table. Those present were outstanding personages who had lived on earth at one time or another. Each one had contributed in a major way toward keeping the true intent of Jesus' ministry before men. Some were martyrs. The differences in their clothing enabled me to determine the various periods and locales in which they had lived. Each one present stood up, in turn, and related the intensely interesting story of his experiences on earth, and of his seeking to preserve the Light and to serve the Lord. A vibrant continuity flowed from one story to another—and I knew that the central theme would continue in dramas yet to be lived by inspired individuals in the ages to come. I also knew that each story, when combined with the others, was building toward a Greater Story. On awakening, I could recall only a portion of one of the stories. This portion had been portrayed on a large screen on a wall—a screen used to project certain parts or vital incidents in each story.

The "W" relates to the Worthy Ones or Saints who have fulfilled the Word through Works. This dream is experienced within the sixth veil of the dream world, where dwell the records of the true Saints' actions. You were perceiving how the thread of good works is immortal and kept alive. When one reaches toward a spiritual life, through training and preparation he may, in time, observe these sacred records of the true Saints. In this manner, he prepares for his own works of worthiness on earth. In some instances in dream experience, a screen is used to portray the dream dramas. This occurs so that the one dreaming may better recall the experience as to detail in symbol and significance.

I dreamed of a woman who, in physical life, is an avid student of metaphysics; however, the corners of her mouth have a tendency to turn downward, giving one the impression that she is perpetually dissatisfied. In the dream I saw that this facial characteristic originated in one of her past lives when she was a male merchant in the Middle East several hundred years ago. In the former life as a merchant the person had deliberately developed this facial expression in dealing with others; for the merchant had learned that, when he looked displeased at his customer's first offer of trade, his grimace would influence the transaction and result in a more profitable trade. This dream impressed upon me the fact that each thing in life has a reason, and that negative or positive characteristics are carried over into a future life or lives.

In this dream you penetrated the fourth dream veil and researched an "embodiment record" of this particular person. One may sometimes research and define in dreams the unexplained defects and frailties in an individual, especially if the life-threads cross in day-time experience as relating to the spiritual life. As a disciple evolves into more awareness and perception,

Ann Ree conducting the first Guild of Ethics, November 1, 1956. Glendale, California.

The Holy Family. Design for a mosaic mural (1959).

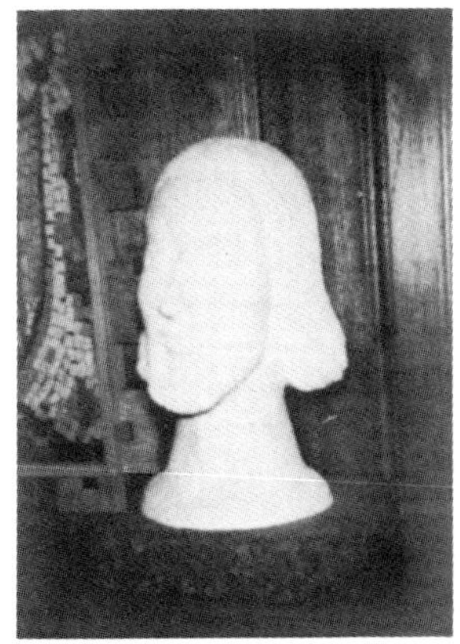

Sculptured head of Jesus, titled "*But I Say Unto You.*" By Ann Ree, 1956.

The Garment of Jesus. Painted by Ann Ree, 1957. Design for a mosaic mural (86″ x 70″) in the Glendale chapel.

Ann Ree with four of the Niscience Lay Ministers.

In the garden at Foundation Headquarters in Glendale, California.

Ann Ree christening Eleanor "Liebschien" Muusmann, 1963.

July 1963. Ann Ree Colton and Jonathan Murro in Santa Barbara, California. Behind them is the glide-swing used at Wooded Place in 1953.

Ann Ree teaching the *Dear Child Round Table* (Glendale, 1964).

dreams and visions of this kind may occur more frequently. In this manner, he comes to develop charitable attitudes toward those near and by. In the above dream, this knowledge is given to the one dreaming so that he may better help the person through his prayers. The disciple may be shown such things in dreams so as to fortify himself in associating with people, and to better understand the hidden motives in the actions of people. The above dream shows that the person dreamed about has retained the defect of cunning, which now stands between her and a spiritual life; and that she would seek to purchase a spiritual life rather than exert the effort to qualify for and earn a spiritual life.

I dreamed of seeing an impressive exhibit of exquisite dishes, vases, and many other objects. A new type of material, unlike any of the materials commonly used today, gave a different texture to these familiar household articles, combining artistry with utility. The objects on display had a distinct quality and novel practicality, in that they were attractive in color and design, unbreakable, and light in weight. The colors of red, yellow, bronze, gold, and copper were brilliant, yet inoffensive. No external coloring was necessary, as the colors seemed to be within and part of the remarkable material of which the objects were constructed. Each piece in the exhibit had a slightly different color pattern, but the colors remained the same.

Mankind is entering a new era of splendor as to music, art, and architecture. Those who enter the higher dream veils may research the coming splendor of this new era. All truly dedicated creators have access, in the waking state or in the dream state, to an uninterrupted stream of creative ideas. These ideas, yet to manifest in the physical world, may be perceived on certain "pre-manifestation" levels in the higher worlds. There they hover over the earth, awaiting the ripe timing for mankind to receive them. New or virginal inventions and formulas for new ideas are reflected from the higher blueprint or archetypal worlds, and may be encountered by persons either through inspiration, vision, or dream. This is the reason why more than one person may lay claim to the same idea at the same time.

The higher one ascends in the dream veils, the more he may relate himself to finer degrees of light and, therefore, to color. Many persons dream in color, unaware that colors carry a symbology telling a story of their own. The colors in the above dream, being inoffensive, indicate that the one dreaming penetrated the higher levels of the fourth dream veil. Each color seen in a dream has meaning and significance. A clear yellow, untinged by any other color, relates to certain expansive powers. Gold relates to spiritual alchemy, and, also, to a solar energy and insulation. Copper symbolizes love among men in the world. The emphasis on such colors in this dream indicates that men are to place their mental powers into action, expanding them through the solar energies. This will result in a closer rapport among peoples of the world. A greater range of color is to be produced, due to the affiliation between art and science. Men are to be more daring in their use of color and in the combining of colors. Thus, they will extend the range of their intellect and emotions.

In a dream I was part of a group gathered around a medical doctor. The doctor, about forty years of age, was speaking to the group. He impressed me as being a very kind person. I thought that if I ever needed an operation I would like to have him do it. I awakened refreshed.

In this dream you were observing a Night Server and his technique in the Night Healing Ministry. The doctor in the dream is a surgeon in the physical world. He is one of many dedicated medical persons who are free to work within the higher dream veils in their everlasting or higher etheric bodies. Such physicians, who serve in the Night Healing Ministry, sustain the true ethic within the medical practice of physical healing, and produce new medical healing techniques in the physical world. This does not mean, however, that all Night Servers must be physicians, for there are many highly evolved persons who are qualified to serve and heal in the Night Ministry. Such dedicated Night Servers are able to release themselves from their physical bodies during sleep and to work with mankind, devoting their night hours to serving the weak and the helpless in the world. As a result of their silent, unclaiming serving in the night, certain individuals may receive preventive, healing helps, or be sustained and strengthened in trials and sicknesses.

A dream is more than unconscious or subconscious fantasy. There is a vital consciousness expressed in dreams. It is possible in sleep to be the recipient of restorative, healing helps, which prevent future sicknesses. This has been experienced by many who understand the validity of the soul's action during sleep.

A person, working harmoniously with his soul in the dream veils, may be instantaneously healed during the hours of sleep through the intermediary action of Night Servers. It is possible in the night hours to be assisted by a mighty company of Night Servers, and to feel not only the joy of renewal and revitalization from such dream experience, but to know that one is sustained through all human circumstances and events.

The many mantrams written by Ann Ree include a number of *Pre-Sleep Mantrams:*

May I work with the tender, healing angels on this night.

* *

At sunset time I turn my face to soul horizons. My soul knoweth where I go on this night, and I know that I shall fare well with my soul.

* *

If I have failed to answer kindness with kindness today, I pray for forgiveness, with rectification on the morrow.

* *

When sleep falls unto me, the claims of the day will cease to bind me, for in the night I am free to immerse my heart in the renewing pool of God's perfect peace.

* *

I would look into the Kingdom on this night, and remember its rapture on the morn.

* *

There are three secret doors to my grace or sacred reserve. They are the door of trying, the door of good intent, and the door of love.

If there be anyone who has shared his crisis with me today, may the healing helps of the angels open my insight; may my prayers become winged messengers—helping, strengthening.

While in Sausalito, California, from July to October 1960, Ann Ree wrote the book *Men in White Apparel.* She felt it necessary to write this book because "there is so much confusion and misunderstanding about life after death; this subject, which is so important to every person, is either ignored, or is handled with indelicate awkwardness."

I prayed that I might show the mercy and grace aspects of death, and reveal the difference between healthy and unhealthy telepathies from the dead.

Men In White Apparel *was written for those who have lost loved ones by death, and to prepare persons for their own dying. To write this book I drew upon ancient death-ritual knowledge from former lives, and knowledge gathered from my research in the present life.*

Men In White Apparel *carries a note of warning to those who would intrude upon or tamper with the sacred precincts of the dead.*

As there is an ethic for the living, there is also an ethic for the dead. When men come to know this ethic, there will be less fear of death and less mystery concerning death.

For three years Ann Ree ignored her heart condition and continued to fulfill each part of her ministry. In December 1961, she became critically ill—and feeling that there was much yet to be done in her work, she prayed that her body might be made whole. One day, while praying and weeping, she heard the voice of Jesus; He spoke into her right ear and asked, "Woman, why weepest thou?" The vibration of His voice penetrated her heart and soul, and she came to peace with her suffering. From this time on, she ceased to resist her sickness, and placed herself in God's Will.

Two weeks later Ann Ree lay close to death in a hospital. X-rays revealed that she had three major coronary scars. Other tests prompted a heart specialist to predict, "She'll never make it." Her regular physician also felt that there was no hope. Her doctor could not understand her reaction to his gloomy prognosis, for she accepted her fate with joy.

When I visited Ann Ree, she said: "I have been close to death for a long time, and I have prolonged my allotment of life. I have no physical or spiritual regrets. I rest in the Father's Will, in His divine Love.

"I feel the soaring of the angels' wings. They are brilliant, dazzling with light. They overdwell me. I am now close to being equal with the angels. It is joyous.

"There have been times, cross-ways, and confusions—but there has been one Light, which has never forsaken me. Sometimes I did almost lose my grasp. The cord between my soul, my heart, my mind and God is one. No longer must I hang upon the cord; I am of the cord.

"What more can one say when he is dying than, 'God's Will be done?' What more can one do than surrender himself to the most divine flame of eternal life?

"There is a divine elegancy to dying, a singular autocracy ordained of God."

The next day Ann Ree experienced ten of the twelve "death ecstasies" that occur to those who have penetrated the Third Heaven. For two hours she spoke in exquisite poetry. On completion of the tenth death ecstasy, she knew that she had been granted *longevity grace,* and that she would live to fulfill her ministry. When I visited her, she said: "On the 12th of December the prototypal shell of the just previous life left me. On the 24th of December my daemon-shadow or dweller left me. On the 26th of December these words were said to me, 'You are now entering the sunrise of your spirit.' On the 29th of December I experienced a perfect uniting, eye to eye, with my Luminosity or Death Angel. I arose into an ecstatic death experience in which I experienced poetry and music. All things were illumined; they were shown to me as they are, rather than as they seem to be."

Ann Ree added two comments for me to read during the forthcoming New Year's Eve service: "There are two time levels. One is the spiritual time-level, and one is the physical time-level. When you can coordinate these perfectly, you are in a state of grace.

"The Holy Ghost is beyond genius. The power of the Holy Ghost uses genius as a handmaiden. And when all the little hardened shells of egotism have been consumed by the fires of genius, Holy Ghost can do His perfect work."

In the ensuing days Ann Ree gained steadily in strength. Those who prayed for her recovery saw their prayers answered.

There is an unknown and mysterious element in healing. The Great Physician was the master of this unknown element—and some in the world have inherited the mantle of spiritual healing.

Faith generates a mysterious alchemy little understood by those who use it daily and constantly.

On Palm Sunday 1962, Ann Ree conducted a number of christenings in the Glendale chapel. Before leaving for Carmel, California in July, she received guidance to prepare *The Venerable One* for publication. The wisdom of this guidance soon proved itself, as the manuscript contained many healing passages that aided in her recuperation.

For *The Venerable One,* Ann Ree selected and edited portions from her diaries of telepathic experiences with the Venerable One in the Great Sierras, in the Great Smokies, and in New York City. While working on this book in Carmel, she returned to "a pure soul-state, so that those who read it might also return to a pure soul-state." She said: "This book is a healing book for me. I had to prepare it in the environment of Nature, where the air is pure and where my eyes can fall on a vision of symmetrical harmony and perfect peace."

After returning to Glendale in November 1962, Ann Ree continued to fulfill her ministry as founder of Niscience. One evening, during a meeting of the members of the Guild of Ethics, she spoke the following mantrams:

Each growing thing
Came to this earth
From another eternity.
Nothing dies in the World of God,
And all Worlds are Worlds of God.
The plant is deathless from eternity to eternity.
How much greater is the life within the soul of man
And the restoring life within his heart?
Let us be quickened
With the restoring life,
That we may earn
The resurrection powers,
The manifestation powers,
And become creators for God.
If our visions are true
And our love selfless,
And our stewardship ethical,
We shall earn these things.

There are Starry Angels loaned to this earth
To remind us
Of other eternities.
Let us look into man
And see from whence he came,
And believe on that which takes him
To his eternal home.

If there be true image,
It cannot fail.
If there be false image
It will destroy itself.

Let us look only into the true image
And become manifestors of the pure.
O Christ,
Thou eternal Son of God,
We turn our lighted bodies unto Thee
And restore
The illumination powers
Of our souls.
May our vision be open.
And may we keep close to the Revelation Angel
And the power reminding us
That we are eternal
With immortal powers.

The versatility of the true initiate, the articulateness of the illumined teacher, the timeless vision of the anointed prophet, and the genuine love of the dedicated masterbuilder—these have been expressed by Ann Ree throughout her ministry. Heaven has placed upon her shoulders a tremendous responsibility—the responsibility of establishing a new spiritual teaching, an advanced teaching, a pure teaching. With the blessings of God, she is accomplishing this difficult objective.

The illumination experienced by Ann Ree—due to her alignment with the Niscience Archetype—has resulted in a prolific quantity and rare quality of creative works. In addition to writing thousands of pages on the System of Niscience, she has delivered hundreds of lectures and sermons; has painted a number of paintings; has worked on beautiful mosaics; has composed inspirational music; has produced works of sculpture;

has written invaluable books; has established a vital Lay Ministry. Her spiritual healing formulas have brought healing to many persons, and her reverent words and works have inspired others "to create, and to serve God."

The worthy works and words of the brilliant System of Niscience add a miraculous leaven to the bread of life, for where they are received they produce much joy, love, and understanding.

In the world today the higher natures of men are rarely cultivated. The lesser nature remains a tenacious taskmaster, until the higher nature begins to awaken and to become the determiner of one's destiny. Gently and wisely, Niscience inspires one to cultivate his higher nature; and, in a relatively short period of time, the radiance of his true self begins to be revealed. The marvel of the higher nature becomes the miracle of the spiritual nature—and one's innate goodness, warmth and magnanimity begin to manifest their fullness for the glory of God.

Life is so very wondrous. How much more wondrous is the spiritual life—the heart at one with God! The spiritual life of Ann Ree Colton is a testimony to the efficacy of prayer and the power of love; a selfless life of serving that has produced its own unique rewards; a reverent life devoted to the principles and ethics of the Lord Jesus; a creative life in which holy grace has freely flowed—thereby producing a bountiful harvest of inestimable good, which this age and future ages will inherit.

May the Presences of Heaven, who call her "daughter," continue to light the pathway before her.

May they continue to endow her with the blessings which come to noble and courageous pioneers of the Spirit.

In August 1963, several of Ann Ree's beloved students from San Francisco came to Carmel to honor her on her birthday. After the dusk devotional service, Ann Ree spoke the following words:

> A birthday is a sacred day. It is the day in which one unites himself with the agreement of his soul. On this day his soul reminds him that he has made a covenent to come into the world. On one's birthday, he should send his gratitude for the loving ones he has contacted throughout life, and for those who have made up the diadem of his living and evolving.
>
> All birthdays are recorded in Heaven. When a birthday is accompanied by a holy festival, it is a special time of anointing. The Cherubim Angels resound the soul-name of a person on his birthday; and, if the heart will hear, one will experience a sacred birthday.
>
> Each person is born in the world with a purpose. If he has fulfilled this purpose with integrity and honor—and especially if he has fulfilled it under the mantle of love—he has left something to the world, something which lives on in the world. On a birthday the soul enables one to look into the births to come, in which he may serve better, and know more, and therefore contribute more to God.

THE END

Index

A

B

D

E

H

I

J

K

L

N

O

P

T

U

V

W

Y